THE PURE THEORY OF INTERNATIONAL TRADE UNDER UNCERTAINTY

The Pure Theory of International Trade Under Uncertainty

Raveendra N. Batra
Southern Methodist University

First published 1975 by
THE MACMILLAN PRESS LTD
London and Basingstoke

*Associated companies in New York Dublin
Melbourne Johannesburg and Madras*

*Distributed in the United States
by Halsted Press, a Division of
John Wiley & Sons, Inc., New York*

SBN 333 16560 8

Library of Congress Catalog Card No. 74–4820

*Filmset by Thomson Litho, East Kilbride,
Scotland*

Printed in Great Britain by
REDWOOD BURN LTD
Trowbridge & Esher

TO MY PARENTS

Contents

Preface

The analysis of economic behaviour under uncertainty is currently recognised to be one of the most productive areas of economics. The scope of the application of the theory of uncertainty in general to various areas of economics is vast, because relatively little has been accomplished despite the fact that individual economic behaviour generally occurs in a stochastic milieu.

Several areas of economic theory are at present being reformulated to take into account the random nature of the economic environment. A good deal of work is under way to integrate uncertainty with the theory of the firm, general equilibrium theory, the theory of consumer behaviour, welfare economics, and so on. The theory of international trade, however, seems to have been untouched by this new and timely wave, although one may legitimately argue that the exposure of a closed economy to international trade contributes more than anything else to uncertainty. In general, international trade introduces in the economy elements that are beyond the control of trading partners.

The purpose of my book is to fill this gap. Specifically, I have made a modest endeavour to blend the recent developments in the stochastic theory of the firm with some ageless issues which have been customarily investigated in terms of the certainty models of international trade.

The plan of the book is this. In the nature of the analysis, the first, introductory chapter is devoted to the development of certain definitions, concepts, and the tools of what may be called probabilistic economics. These tools are then utilised to analyse the input–output decision-making of a competitive firm operating in a stochastic environment.

It is not an exaggeration to say that the foundations of the modern theory of international trade rest on the basic characteristics of the deterministic, two-sector, two-factor, constant returns to scale, general equilibrium model of production. Accordingly, the second chapter is concerned with the formulation of a stochastic, two-by-two, general equilibrium model.

The properties of the framework developed in Chapter 2 are then utilised in the next three chapters to examine the validity of the Heckscher–Ohlin theory of the pattern of trade as well as the factor-price equalisation theorem.

Chapter 6 deals with the resource allocational and income-distribution impact of the stabilisation of international prices of primary products, and Chapter 7 with the implications of uncertainty for social welfare. Finally, Chapter 8 contains some suggestions for future research.

In the past, the evolution of international economics has contributed munificently to the progress achieved in several other areas of economics, notably public finance, labour economics, economic growth and regional economics. The two-sector model of international trade has been the principal conduit of this contribution. It is my hope that the stochastic two-by-two framework developed in this book will also have interesting and important ramifications for other fields of economic theory where the applications of uncertainty have so far been ignored.

The lack of complexity of the models developed in this book may come as a pleasant surprise to the reader. True, the method of analysis is predominantly algebraic, but the reader needs no more than a working knowledge of elementary calculus and statistics. In general, those who have some understanding of the techniques of total and partial differentiation will find the book intelligible after reading the introductory chapter. Wherever possible, the algebraic argument has been supplemented by intuitive explications as well as diagrams.

In writing this book, I have benefited considerably from the generous suggestions from my colleagues, Professors William R. Russell and Josef Hadar. Indeed, they are to be blamed for getting me interested in the theory of economic behaviour under uncertainty. I also wish to express my gratitude to Dr Aman Ullah for allowing me to include parts of our joint article in the first chapter.

I take this opportunity to thank Professor M. C. Kemp, whose suggestions on one of my articles led to the development of section 2.10, which deals with the case of joint products. I should also like to express my gratitude to my students, Jungshik Son, Parthasarathi

Shome and Sandwip Das, for patient and attentive reading of various drafts of this book. I am indebted to indefatigable Becky Haire for quick, precise typing of all these drafts.

Finally, I should like to acknowledge my great debt to Professor Jagdish Bhagwati for creating and sustaining my interest in the pure theory of international trade. To Southern Methodist University, I owe a heavy debt of gratitude for providing me with excellent research facilities. Last but not least, the credit for drawing the diagrams goes as usual to my artist wife, Diane.

Dallas, Texas   RAVEENDRA N. BATRA
August 1973

PART 1   Production Uncertainty

1   Introduction

1.1   Introduction

Almost every mode of economic behaviour is influenced by uncertainty. The farmer faces uncertainty about weather as well as the product price; the entrepreneur in a mechanised industry is not affected that much by the vagaries of weather, but he may have to cope with the vagaries of his employees, plant breakdown or even the possibilities of a strike; the number of customers coming to a store on any day is random; at the country level, the foreign demand for its products may be stochastic, or the foreign supply of raw materials may be random. Thus, uncertainty affects virtually every aspect of economic life. Yet, it is only recently that the economist has begun to analyse the economic decision-making of individuals under conditions of uncertainty. In view of the general stochastic nature of the economic milieu, it is not easy to explain the long neglect of integration with deterministic economic models of the theory of probability, which furnishes the analytical tools needed to investigate the individual behaviour under a probabilistic economic environment.

For a long time, statistics and economics were regarded as completely different disciplines. The statistician would not get entrapped in the web of the economist's logic, and the economist would not come out of the sanctuary of untested theoretical models. Recently, the tools of statistics have been integrated with those of economics into what is widely called econometrics, yet this integration has been only partial. A more complete blending is yet to be accomplished, and the development of probabilistic economics constitutes another step in this direction.

Perhaps the most important reason for the dearth of literature in earlier probabilistic economic theory is the erroneous but widely held belief that most of the results of the deterministic (non-stochastic) model remain essentially unscathed when random elements are incorporated into the analysis. The belief is: Instead of using actual values, use expected values of the variables. If the explicit incorporation of the stochastic elements in the conventional certainty models results only in minor modifications to the established results, serious objections may be raised against the use of the probabilistic approach, which inevitably gives rise to labyrinthine mathematical calculations. In general, the stochastic solutions to economic problems are radically different from their certainty counterparts, and even in cases where the results remain qualitatively the same, the derivation of the proofs requires special care and, sometimes, controversial assumptions. This, indeed, has been the experience of the majority of economists who have in recent years attempted to explore the implications of uncertainty for results derived from deterministic models. The conclusions that emerge from the present study turn out to be no different, as we shall see in the subsequent chapters.

One striking result that has been obtained by a number of authors investigating the theory of the firm under uncertainty is that the risk-averse firm employs smaller quantities of factors and hence produces a lower output than the firm operating under certainty conditions, because the former hires inputs in such a way that the expected value of the marginal product of the factor exceeds the input price, whereas in a non-stochastic environment, the profit-maximising competitive firm equates the value of the input's marginal product with the input price. This latter result lies at the heart of most conventional international trade models. However, when the firm, operating in the stochastic environment, makes optimal input-hiring decisions by not equating the expected marginal value productivity of the factor to the factor price, the basic results of international trade theory may also be modified. This emerges clearly from our analysis in the latter chapters.

The present chapter is concerned with developing the tools of analysis, which enable us to analyse the behaviour of the competitive firm under uncertainty.

1.2   The von Neumann–Morgenstern Utility Function

The basic problem in designing probabilistic models to cope with uncertainty is that one need not only take into account the expected values of the random variables and hence allow for the probabilities involved, but the decision-maker's attitude towards risk must also be taken into consideration. In deciding whether to manufacture a new product, for example, the producer must have some idea of the expected demand for the product as well as its expected cost of production. This requires a subjective assessment, on the part of the producer, of the various probabilities attaching to the possible values of the uncertain variables.

In order to determine the extent of the manufacturer's investment in the new venture, or to find if it will ever be undertaken, we must not only assume knowledge on the part of the 'rational' producer of the (subjective) probability distributions of the unknown variables, but we must also know whether the producer has aversion, indifference, or preference for the risk involved in the possibility of loss from the new project.

A simple method to deal with these problems is suggested by the von Neumann–Morgenstern utility theory, which is closely related to the probability theory. This approach, however, rests on various behavioural postulates, implicit in a set of axioms underlying the existence of the von Neumann–Morgenstern utility function. The acceptance of this utility function implies approbation of these axioms, which were lucidly explained originally by von Neumann and Morgenstern [15] and later by DeGroot [4], Ferguson [5] and Horowitz [9]. As Horowitz points out, taken individually, these axioms appear to be innocuous, but taken together, they are strong and restrictive assumptions. As with the analyses of many recent writers, our approach is subject to this limitation.

Once we accept the existence of a utility function, the formal characterisation of the decision-maker's risk attitude in terms of the properties of the utility function can be easily accomplished. Suppose the utility function of wealth, x,

$$U(x) \tag{1.1}$$

is differentiable up to the third order, with $U'(x) > 0$ implying that utility is strictly increasing in wealth, where $U'(x)$, the first derivate of the function $U(x)$, is the marginal utility from wealth. If $U(x)$ satisfies the axioms of the von Neumann–Morgenstern utility theory, then the sign of the second derivate of $U(x)$, $U''(x)$, determines the wealth holder's attitude towards risk. Specifically, if $U''(x) = 0$, so that the utility function is linear, the wealth holder is indifferent, neutral, or apathetic towards risk; if $U''(x) < 0$, so that the utility function is strictly concave, the individual is risk-averse; finally, if

$U''(x) > 0$, so that the utility function is strictly convex, the individual is risk-preferrent.

It is usually assumed that individuals evince aversion towards risk. Arrow argues that the von Neumann–Morgenstern utility function must be bounded from above, which means that the individual is normally a risk-averter. It should be emphasised, however, that the case of risk-preference creates no additional analytical problems. Furthermore, $U''(x)$ is definitely negative only in the range below the upper bound of $U(x)$. Therefore, if x is limited to finite values, $U''(x)$ may be positive.

1.3   The Arrow–Pratt Risk-Aversion Functions

Probabilistic economists have found that the assumptions of $U'(x) > 0$ and $U''(x) < 0$ do not provide sufficient restrictions on the utility function. What happens to risk-aversion (or even risk-preference) as the individual's wealth increases? It may appear that the direction of the change in $U''(x)$ is an appropriate measure of risk-aversion. However, the utility function is unique up to a linear transformation, whereas $U''(x)$ is not, and it has been argued that a satisfactory measure of risk-aversion should have this property of uniqueness.† Arrow [1] and Pratt [11] have introduced a measure of absolute risk-aversion (R_a) which has this uniqueness property. They define R_a as

$$R_a(x) = -\frac{U''(x)}{U'(x)}. \tag{1.2}$$

Another risk-aversion function introduced by Arrow is the relative risk-aversion (R_r) function, which is defined as

$$R_r(x) = -\frac{xU''(x)}{U'(x)} \tag{1.3}$$

Arrow argues that absolute risk-aversion is a non-increasing function of wealth. This hypothesis is quite appealing, because it implies that, as income increases, the individual's willingness to engage in small gambles of a fixed size does not decrease. After all, as the individual gets wealthier, one should normally expect a decline in his risk-aversion or in his risk-premium, which can be defined as the difference between the expected value of the return from the risky

† For further details on this point, see McCall [10, pp. 407–10].

prospect and its certainty equivalent. In the context of a portfolio model, Arrow shows that non-increasing risk-aversion implies that risky investment is not an inferior good. The hypothesis of non-increasing absolute risk-aversion has been widely accepted and, as McCall [10] points out, it has also withstood the empirical tests.

Arrow further argues that the relative risk-aversion is a non-decreasing function of wealth. This implies that if both the size of the bet and wealth are augmented in the same proportion, the willingness to accept the bet does not decrease. In the context of the portfolio model, this hypothesis implies that non-risky investment is a luxury good. The hypothesis of non-decreasing relative risk-aversion lacks the intuitive appeal and the empirical evidence of the hypothesis of non-increasing absolute risk-aversion and, therefore, has not gained wide currency. In the subsequent chapters, we utilise the hypothesis of non-increasing absolute risk-aversion, but because of its controversial nature, ignore the concept of the relative risk-aversion function.

1.4 Definition of an Increase in Riskiness or Uncertainty

An interesting question in probabilistic economics concerns the implications of a marginal change in riskiness or uncertainty. For this type of analysis, we must first agree on a self-consistent and intuitively appealing definition of a change in the degree of uncertainty. One measure of riskiness which suggests itself is the variance of the random variable. In some circumstances, however, the variance becomes a self-contradictory measure of uncertainty.†
Working independently, Hadar and Russell [7] and Rothschild and Stiglitz [12, 13] analysed the general problem of ordering uncertain prospects and the measurement of risk. The measure of riskiness that we utilise in this book has been called by Rothschild and Stiglitz a 'mean-preserving spread'. In this measure, a small increase in

† Another objection which has been frequently voiced against the use of variance as a measure of risk concerns the use of the mean-variance approach with which this measure is invariably associated. In the mean-variance analysis, the decision-maker facing risk is assumed to be aware of efficiency frontiers between the expected value of the random variable and its variance. However, the efficiency frontier of the mean-variance hypothesis is not necessarily equivalent to that of the expected utility approach. Furthermore, the mean-variance analysis is invariably illustrated with the aid of a quadratic utility function, which has an objectionable property in that it gives rise to an absolute risk-aversion function which is a strictly increasing function of wealth. And we have already argued above that the absolute risk-aversion is realistically a non-increasing function of wealth.

riskiness or uncertainty is defined by the stretching of the original density function of the random variable around a constant mean.

Let A and B be two random variables with similar means; then B is 'more risky' than A if the probability distribution of B has longer tails than the probability distribution of A. The 'more risky' distribution of B can be obtained from the distribution of A by removing the probability mass away from the density function of A and towards the tails in such a way that the mean remains the same. For example, consider Fig. 1.1, where the bell-shaped curve aa represents the density function of A, and the dotted curve bb represents the density function of B. The curve bb has been obtained by spreading

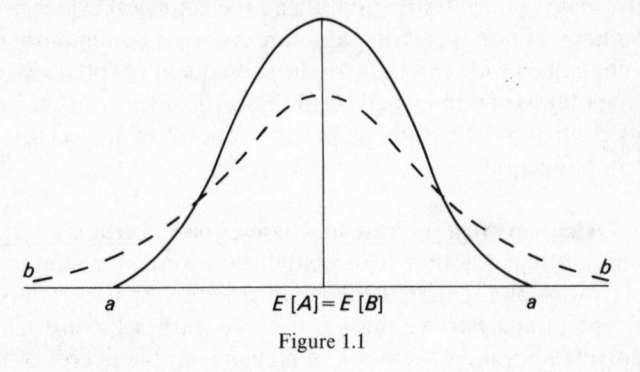

Figure 1.1

the density function of A – curve aa – such that the mean of A, equal to $E[A]$, is unchanged. The transformation of aa into bb is called the mean-preserving spread. This measure of riskiness suggests that if curve aa is replaced by curve bb, then there occurs an increase in risk or uncertainty, and conversely.

In some subsequent chapters, the random variable is denoted by α. In terms of the mean-preserving spread, the increase in riskiness may be defined in this way. Let us write $\hat{\alpha}$ as

$$\hat{\alpha} = \gamma\alpha + \theta$$

where γ and θ are shift parameters, and initially $\gamma = 1$ and $\theta = 0$. The variance of $\hat{\alpha}$, $v(\hat{\alpha})$, is given by

$$v(\hat{\alpha}) = v(\alpha)\gamma^2$$

where $v(\alpha)$ is the variance of α. The expected value of $\hat{\alpha}$, on the other hand, is given by

$$E[\hat{\alpha}] = \gamma E[\alpha] + \theta.$$

It is clear now that an increase in γ above its initial value of unity leads to an increase in the variance as well as the expected value of $\hat{\alpha}$, whereas a rise in θ above its initial level of zero causes only a rise in $E[\hat{\alpha}]$. Thus, in order to restore the original mean of $\hat{\alpha}$, an increase in γ should be matched by a decline in θ by an amount such that $dE[\hat{\alpha}] = 0$, or

$$dE[\hat{\alpha}] = E[\alpha]d\gamma + d\theta = 0$$

so that

$$\frac{d\theta}{d\gamma} = -E[\alpha].$$

An increase in uncertainty in terms of the mean-preserving spread is then defined by $d\gamma > 0$ and $d\theta/d\gamma = -E[\alpha]$.

1.5 Behaviour of the Competitive Firm Under Uncertainty

The earlier sections of this chapter have been devoted to the development of certain concepts by means of which one can analyse the behaviour of any particular decision-maker facing risky situations. In this section, we apply these concepts to investigate the behaviour of a competitive firm operating under stochastic circumstances. Uncertainty in the deterministic competitive model of the firm may be incorporated in a variety of plausible ways. The firm may be uncertain about the price at which it will be able to sell its product, or there may be uncertainty in the production function where the supply of the finished product may be sensitive to factors beyond the firm's control, and so on. In the following, we develop a two-input model of the competitive firm which regards the level of its finished product to be stochastic. Results are qualitatively unmodified, if the firm were uncertain about the product price.

Consider a competitive firm which takes its product price, p, and factor prices as exogenously given and which is interested in maximising the expected utility from profits, π, where

$$\pi = pX - wL - rK \tag{1.4}$$

where X is the product, L and K denote respectively the inputs of labour and capital, and w and r are, respectively, the wage-rate and the rental of capital. The production function of the firm is given by

$$X = \alpha F(K, L) \tag{1.5}$$

where α is a random variable with a probability distribution, $G(\alpha)$, a density function, $g(\alpha)$ and a mean value, $E[\alpha] = \mu$, where E is the expectations operator.† Thus, the production function is assumed to be multiplicatively separable in a random variable and a non-stochastic function, F; α could represent the influence of weather, the possibility of accidental fires, plant breakdowns, industrial strikes and any other factor which is beyond the control of the management and which makes the actual level of the finished product, X, uncertain. Furthermore, $\alpha > 0$ and $\partial X/\partial \alpha > 0$, that is, α contributes to output in the same way as non-random inputs. Since the firm has no say in the determination of α, the distribution of α is exogenously given. In addition, we assume that production and hence input-hiring decisions have to be made prior to the resolution of α.

In view of (1.5), profit becomes

$$\pi = p\alpha F(K,L) - wL - rK. \tag{1.6}$$

The firm is interested in maximising

$$E[U] = E[U(\pi)] = \int_\alpha U(pX - wL - rK)g(\alpha)d\alpha \tag{1.7}$$

with respect to its two decision variables, L and K. This maximisation is accomplished by partially differentiating (1.7) with respect to L and K, and setting the derivatives to zero.‡ Thus, given that the differentiation of expected values is permitted, the first-order conditions for the maximum are

$$\frac{\partial E[U]}{\partial L} = E\left[U'(\pi)\frac{\partial \pi}{\partial L}\right] = E[U'(p\alpha F_L - w)] = 0 \tag{1.8}$$

and

$$\frac{\partial E[U]}{\partial K} = E\left[U'(\pi)\frac{\partial \pi}{\partial K}\right] = E[U'(p\alpha F_K - r)] = 0 \tag{1.9}$$

where $U' \equiv U'(\pi) = dU(\pi)/d\pi$ is the marginal utility from profits and where αF_L and αF_K are, respectively, the marginal products of labour

---

† A more general stochastic production function is given by

$$X = F(K, L, \alpha)$$

but this function turns out to be too general to yield categorical results. For this reason, and owing to the fact that a function like (1.5) has been previously utilised by Bardhan and Srinivasan [2] and Sandmo [14], we are using a less general production function.

‡ The analysis that follows is based on the article by Batra and Aman Ullah [3].

and capital. The second-order conditions for the maximum are given by

$$\frac{\partial^2 E[U]}{\partial L^2} = Q_1 = E[U''(p\alpha F_L - w)^2 + p\alpha F_{LL}U'] < 0 \qquad (1.10)$$

$$\frac{\partial^2 E[U]}{\partial K^2} = Q_2 = E[U''(p\alpha F_K - r)^2 + p\alpha F_{KK}U'] < 0 \qquad (1.11)$$

and

$$Q_1 Q_2 - T^2 = J > 0 \qquad (1.12)$$

where

$$T = \frac{\partial^2 E[U]}{\partial L \partial K} = E[U''(p\alpha F_K - r)(p\alpha F_L - w) + p\alpha F_{KL}U'] > 0$$

$$(1.13)$$

and

$$F_{LL} = \partial F_L/\partial L, \ F_{KK} = \partial F_K/\partial K, \ F_{KL} = \partial F_L/\partial K \text{ and } U'' = dU'/d\pi.$$

Let us now examine the requirements of the second-order conditions for the attainment of maximum expected utility. In the certainty case, utility maximisation on the part of the firm requires that

$$F_{ii} < 0 \quad \text{and} \quad (F_{LL}F_{KK} - F_{KL}^2) > 0 \qquad (i = L, K)$$

which means that the production function is strictly concave.† We will now show that if the firm is risk-averse, so that $U'' < 0$, strict concavity of the production function is sufficient, but not necessary, to ensure expected utility maximisation.

Expanding (1.12) by using (1.10), (1.11) and (1.13), we obtain

$$J = \{E[U''a^2]E[U''h^2] - (E[U''ah])^2\} + \{E[p\alpha U'](F_{KK}E[U''a^2]$$
$$+ F_{LL}E[U''h^2]) - 2F_{KL}E[U''ah]\}$$
$$+ E[p\alpha U'](F_{LL}F_{KK} - F_{KL}^2) \qquad (1.14)$$

where $a \equiv p\alpha F_L - w$ and $h \equiv p\alpha F_K - r$. From the first-order conditions (1.8) and (1.9), since F_i is non-random, and since the competitive firm takes w and r as given,

$$\frac{w}{r} = \omega = \frac{pF_L E[\alpha U']}{pF_K E[\alpha U']} = \frac{F_L}{F_K}. \qquad (1.15)$$

---

† See, for instance, Henderson and Quandt [8, pp. 61–69] for a clear-cut statement of these conditions.

Using this in a and h, we get

$$a = (p\alpha F_L - w) = \frac{F_L}{F_K}(p\alpha F_K - r) = \omega h$$

so that $a^2 = \omega^2 h^2$. Using this, the first term in (1.14) reduces to zero and J becomes

$$J = -\frac{E[U''h^2]}{F_L^2}(2F_L F_K F_{KL} - F_L^2 F_{KK} - F_K^2 F_{LL})$$
$$+ E[p\alpha U'](F_{LL}F_{KK} - F_{KL}^2). \tag{1.16}$$

For second-order conditions to be satisfied, Q_1 and Q_2 from (1.10) and (1.11) should be negative, whereas J should be positive. If the firm is risk-averse, then $U'' < 0$, in which case Q_1 and Q_2 may be negative even if F_{LL} and F_{KK} are positive. This immediately suggests that the function F need not be concave for (1.10) and (1.11) to be satisfied. This also holds true for (1.12), for from (1.16), J may be positive even if $(F_{LL}F_{KK} - F_{KL}^2) < 0$, provided, of course, that iso-quants are convex to the origin, so that

$$2F_L F_K F_{KL} - F_L^2 F_{KK} - F_K^2 F_{LL} > 0.\dagger$$

Thus, if the firm is risk-averse, the concavity of the function F is no longer necessary for the attainment of the optimum. However, concavity is sufficient, because it implies a negative F_{ii} as well as convexity of the isoquants towards the origin.

If the firm is risk-neutral, then concavity is both necessary and sufficient for equations (1.10)–(1.12) to be satisfied, because, here, $U'' = 0$. However, if the firm is a risk-preferer, so that $U'' > 0$, then the concavity of the function F becomes a necessary, though not a sufficient condition for the firm to be at the optimum.

Suppose the firm is risk-averse or neutral; then the convexity of the isoquants towards the origin – along with (1.15) – implies that even under uncertainty, the firm minimises the unit cost of produc-tion for whatever expected (or even actual) output it chooses to produce. As with the certainty case, the marginal rate of substitution between the factors (given by $F_L/F_K = -dK/dL$) equals the factor-price ratio at the optimum, even when the firm is operating under an uncertain environment. This is an interesting result, because in what follows we show that the optimal output of the risk-averse firm

† The conditions ensuring convexity of the isoquants are illustrated in many micro-economic textbooks. See, for instance, Hadar [6, pp. 26–27].

is such that the expected marginal value productivity of each factor exceeds the given input price. In other words, the risk-averse firm produces an output at which price exceeds expected marginal cost, but the level of output is one at which the composition of the factors is optimal. Similarly, a risk-preferring firm, given that an optimum exists, also employs an optimal combination of resources, but its expected output is such that its expected marginal cost exceeds the given price.

Let us explore further the case of the risk-averter. From (1.6), expected profit is given by

$$E[\pi] = E[\alpha]pF - wL - rK = \mu pF - wL - rK \qquad (1.17)$$

where $F \equiv F(K,L)$ and $\mu \equiv E[\alpha]$. From (1.17), $wL + rK = \mu pF - E[\pi]$. Substituting for $wL + rK$ in (1.6), we obtain

$$\pi = E[\pi] + (\alpha - \mu)pF \qquad (1.18)$$

so that $\pi \geqslant E[\pi]$ for $\alpha \geqslant \mu$. This means that, if the firm is risk-averse, the marginal utility from profits is lower from π than it is from $E[\pi]$, that is

$$U'(\pi) \leqslant U'(E[\pi]) \qquad \text{for } \alpha \geqslant \mu.$$

Multiplying both sides by $(\alpha - \mu)$ then furnishes

$$U'(\pi)(\alpha - \mu) \leqslant U'(E[\pi])(\alpha - \mu) \qquad \text{for } \alpha \geqslant \mu. \qquad (1.19)$$

This inequality holds also for $\alpha \leqslant \mu$, because then $U'(\pi) \geqslant U'(E[\pi])$, so that multiplying this by $(\alpha - \mu) \leqslant 0$ simply yields (1.19). Applying the expectations operator to both sides of (1.19) then gives

$$E[U'(\pi)(\alpha - \mu)] \leqslant U'(E[\pi])E[\alpha - \mu]$$

because, with $E[\pi]$ being a certain number, $U'(E[\pi])$ is also a certain number.

Now $E[\alpha - \mu] = 0$. Hence,

$$E[U'(\pi)(\alpha - \mu)] \leqslant 0 \qquad (1.20)$$

for the risk-averse firm. From (1.8),

$$E[U'(\pi)p\alpha F_L] = wE[U'(\pi)]. \qquad (1.21)$$

Subtracting $E[U'(\pi)]\mu pF_L$ from both sides of (1.21), we get

$$E[U'(\pi)(\alpha - \mu)]pF_L = E[U'(\pi)](w - \mu pF_L)$$

and since $E[U'(\pi)(\alpha - \mu)]$ is non-positive from (1.20), and since $E[U'(\pi)] > 0$,

$$w \leqslant p\mu F_L. \tag{1.22}$$

The term μF_L is the expected marginal productivity of labour, and $p\mu F_L$ is the value of the expected marginal productivity of labour. Hence, from (1.22), the conclusion is unmistakable: The risk-averse firm employs labour in such a way that the wage rate falls short of the expected marginal value productivity of labour. Since $w/\mu F_L$ is the expected marginal cost of labour, and since, in view of (1.15), $w/\mu F_L = r/\mu F_K$, (1.22) also implies that the price of the competitive firm exceeds its expected marginal cost.

Similarly, we can prove that

$$r \leqslant p\mu F_K$$

for the risk-averter, whereas for the risk-indifferent firm,

$$w = p\mu F_L \quad \text{and} \quad r = p\mu F_K. \tag{1.23}$$

Finally, for the risk preferrer,

$$w \geqslant p\mu F_L \quad \text{and} \quad r \geqslant p\mu F_K.$$

This analysis makes it clear that the behaviour of the risk-neutral firm is similar to the firm's behaviour under a certainty milieu. For example, suppose that the value of α is known to be equal to μ with certainty, then the utility-maximising firm sets

$$U'(\pi)(p\mu F_L - w) \quad \text{and} \quad U'(\pi)(p\mu F_K - r)$$

to zero, and since $U'(\pi) > 0$, $w = p\mu F_L$ and $r = p\mu F_K$, which is identical to (1.23). Thus, the deterministic behaviour of the firm is similar to the behaviour of the risk-neutral firm facing uncertainty.

It must be clear by now that, given that $F_{ii} < 0$, a risk-averse firm employs smaller amounts of inputs than does a risk-neutral firm, so that the expected output of the latter exceeds that of the former. Similarly, the expected output of a risk-preferring firm exceeds even the expected output of the risk-indifferent firm.

Since the behaviour of the risk-apathetic firm can be identified with that of the firm operating under certainty, we conclude that the risk-averse firm produces a smaller, and the risk-preferring firm a larger output than the firm operating under certainty. Note that, in such comparisons, the actual value of α is constrained to the mean of the original distribution, μ, so that the expected and actual outputs of the firms facing uncertainty are the same.

A geometrical demonstration of these results turns out to be very rewarding in terms of clarity and comprehension. Consider Fig. 1.2, where the vertical axis measures the given wage-rate and the value of the expected marginal productivity of labour, i.e. $p\mu F_L$, and the horizontal axis measures the employment of labour, with the curve AB depicting the relationship between the utilisation of labour and its expected marginal value productivity. If α were known with

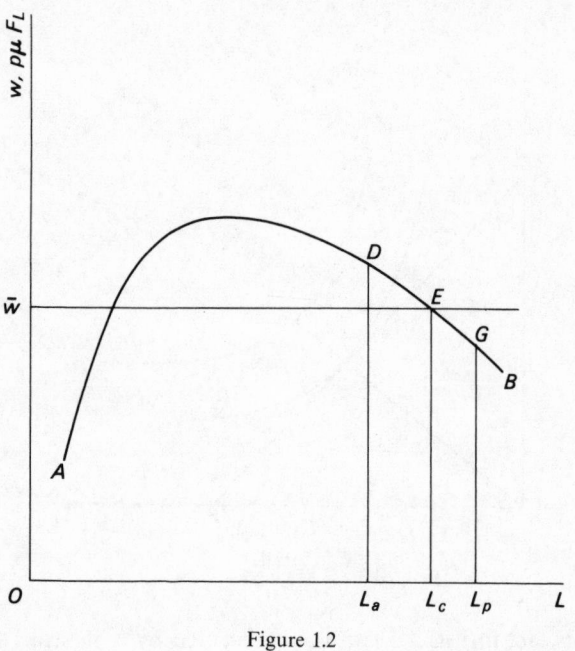

Figure 1.2

certainty to be equal to μ, the competitive firm, facing the given wage rate $\bar{w}$, would hire OL_c amount of labour, because it is only at E that the two conditions for utility maximisation, namely (1) $p\mu F_L = w$, and (2) $F_{LL} < 0$, are satisfied. If the firm is risk-averse, the employment of labour is OL_a, because at a point such as D, $p\mu F_L = DL_a > \bar{w}$ and $F_{LL} < 0$. On the other hand, a risk-preferring firm employs OL_p amount of labour, because at a point such as G, $p\mu F_L = GL_p < \bar{w}$. The ramifications for the output of different types of firms are now straightforward. A similar diagram is also available in relation to the market for capital.

Figure 1.3 translates the data generated by Fig. 1.2 into an isoquant diagram, where, under certainty conditions, AB is the isocost line and x_1 is the unit isoquant representing one unit of output (i.e. $\mu F = 1$), with E being the point of equilibrium generating the optimum capital/labour ratio given by the slope of the ray OE. The quintessence of our analysis of the firm is that when uncertainty is introduced, then for the same levels of w, r and p, the risk-averse firm produces a lower output – given, of course, that α is constrained

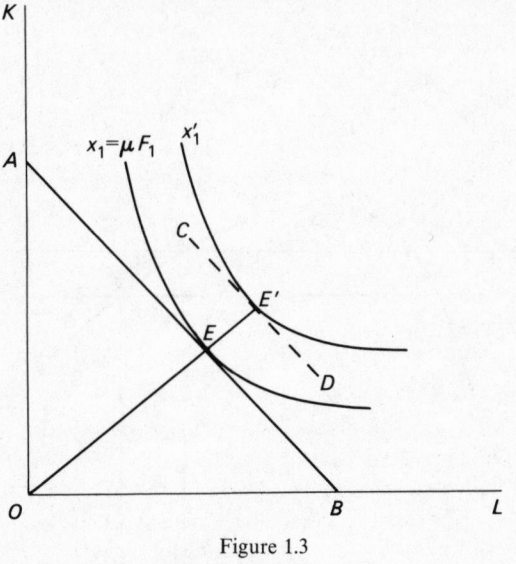

Figure 1.3

to μ. This fact in Fig. 1.3 can be represented by a 'neutral' shift of the unit isoquant away from the origin to x_1'. By a neutral shift, we mean that at the original wage/rental ratio given by the slope of AB, parallel to CD, the optimal capital/labour ratio is unchanged at the slope of the ray OE, so that at the original w, r and p, the output declines from one unit to the level represented by OE/OE'. It is now a simple matter to conclude that the risk-preference case can be represented by a neutral shift (not shown in the diagram) of the unit isoquant towards the origin.

The results derived above can be obtained in yet another way by using what can be termed the covariance method. The covariance between any two random variables, such as $a(\alpha)$ and $b(\alpha)$ is defined as

$$\begin{aligned}
\text{cov}(a, b) &= E\big[(a - E[a])(b - E[b])\big] \\
&= E\Big[ab - aE[b] - E[a]b + E[a]E[b]\Big] \\
&= E[ab] - E[a]E[b] - E[a]E[b] + E[a]E[b] \\
&= E[ab] - E[a]E[b].
\end{aligned}$$

Applying this result to equation (1.21), for example, yields

$$\Big[E[U']\mu + \text{cov}(U', \alpha)\Big]pF_L = wE[U']$$

whence

$$p\mu F_L = w - \frac{\text{cov}(U', \alpha)}{E[U']}. \tag{1.24}$$

The sign of the covariance between U' and α is determined by how U' and α are related. An increase in α contributes to a rise in profit, and if the firms are risk-averse, $U'(\pi)$ will decline. Therefore, for risk-averse firms, the covariance between U' and α is negative. Similarly, for risk-neutral firms the covariance is zero, and for risk-preferring firms it is positive. In the light of this discussion, it is clear from (1.24) that with risk-averse firms

$$w < p\mu F_L$$

a result that has already been derived. Thus, the covariance method is another way of deriving the results concerning individual economic behaviour under uncertainty.

Until now, our analysis has been concerned with the case of uncertainty in the production function. The case where the firm is uncertain about its price, but not output, can be analysed analogously. The analysis by Batra and Aman Ullah [3] deals with the case of price uncertainty where α is assumed to be unity. The results, however, do not differ qualitatively. The output of the risk-averse firm continues to be lower than the certainty output, and so on.

1.6 Summary

This chapter has been concerned with the development of the tools of analysis, which will be utilised extensively to facilitate our exposition of the subsequent chapters. The concepts of expected utility maximisation, the individual's attitude towards risk, the degree of riskiness, etc were developed in the foregoing sections. These concepts were then applied to illustrate the behaviour of the competitive firm encountering uncertainty in its production function or the market price. The general conclusion was that a risk-averse firm produces a lower output, and a risk-preferring firm a higher output than the firm operating in a certainty environment.

Finally, we find it worth stating here that, although the case of the risk-preferring firm has been analysed in this chapter, this case will be referred to only occasionally in the subsequent chapters. The main focus will be on risk-averse behaviour because of its realistic nature, and on the risk-neutrality case because the latter can be identified with the results available from corresponding deterministic models.

REFERENCES

[1] Arrow, K. J., *Essays in the Theory of Risk-Bearing* (Chicago: Markham, 1971) essay 3.

[2] Bardhan, P. K., and Srinivasan, T. N., 'Cropsharing Tenancy in Agriculture: A Theoretical and Empirical Analysis', *American Economic Review*, 61 (Mar 1971) 48–64.

[3] Batra, R. N., and Aman Ullah, 'Competitive Firm and the Theory of Input Demand Under Price Uncertainty', *Journal of Political Economy*, 82 (May–June 1974) 537–48.

[4] DeGroot, M. H., *Optimal Statistical Decisions* (New York: McGraw-Hill, 1970).

[5] Ferguson, T. S., *Mathematical Statistics: A Decision Theoretic Approach* (New York: Academic Press, 1967).

[6] Hadar, J., *Mathematical Theory of Economic Behaviour* (Reading, Mass.: Addison-Wesley, 1971).

[7] Hadar, J., and Russell, W. R., 'Rules for Ordering Uncertain Prospects', *American Economic Review*, 59 (Mar 1969) 25–34.

[8] Henderson, H., and Quandt, R. E., *Microeconomic Theory: A Mathematical Approach* 2nd ed. (New York: McGraw-Hill, 1971).

[9] Horowitz, I., *Decision Making and the Theory of the Firm* (New York: Holt, Rinehart and Winston, 1970).

[10] McCall, J. J., 'Probabilistic Microeconomics', *Bell Journal of Economics and Management Science*, 2 (autumn 1971) 403–33.

[11] Pratt, J. W., 'Risk Aversion in the Small and in the Large', *Econometrica*, 32 (Jan–Apr 1964) 122–36.

[12] Rothschild, M., and Stiglitz, J. E., 'Increasing Risk I: A Definition', *Journal of Economic Theory*, 2 (Sept 1970) 225–43.

[13] ——, 'Increasing Risk II: Its Economic Consequences', *Journal of Economic Theory*, 3 (Mar 1971) 66–84.

[14] Sandmo, A., 'Discount Rates for Public Investment Under Uncertainty', *International Economic Review*, 13 (June 1972) 287–302.

[15] von Neumann, J., and Morgenstern, O., *Theory of Games and Economic Behavior* (Princeton: Princeton University Press, 1947).

SUPPLEMENTARY READINGS

These readings concern recent developments in the theory of the firm under uncertainty.

[16] Baron, D. P., 'Price Uncertainty, Utility and Industry Equilibrium in Pure Competition', *International Economic Review*, 11 (Oct 1970) 463–80.

[17] Sandmo, A., 'On the Theory of the Competitive Firm Under Price Uncertainty', *American Economic Review*, 61 (Mar 1971) 65–73.

[18] Tisdell, C. A., *The Theory of Price Uncertainty, Production and Profit* (Princeton: Princeton University Press, 1968).

2 A General Equilibrium Model of Production Under Uncertainty

The modern deterministic theory of international trade has been built upon the salient characteristics of the two-sector, two-factor, general equilibrium model of production. Therefore, the prerequisite to the development of the stochastic theory of international trade is the formulation of a two-by-two general equilibrium model, which takes into account the random nature of the economic environment. This is the task assigned to this chapter.† In pursuit of this goal, we draw extensively on the analytical tools developed in the previous chapter.

2.1 Assumptions and the Model

Unless otherwise specified, the following assumptions will be maintained throughout the book. A number of these assumptions are the same as those adopted by the certainty model, whereas a few others are introduced to facilitate our exposition of uncertainty.

1. The production activity in the economy can be divided into two sectors, and X_1 and X_2 represent the respective sectors, as well as the levels of output. Each good is produced with the help of two factors, capital (K) and labour (L). The production functions are linearly homogeneous and concave, implying the prevalence of constant returns to scale and diminishing returns to factor proportions.

2. There is perfect competition in all markets; factors are fully employed and inelastically supplied; in addition, factor intensities are non-reversible, that is, the inter-industry factor-intensity relationship is invariant for all factor-price ratios. In addition. factors are perfectly mobile between the two industries. This mobility, of course, becomes relevant only when the X_1 producers have to make input-output decisions; once these decisions are made, factors cannot move from one sector to

† The model developed in this chapter is based on the one formulated by Batra [2].

the other even if economic conditions change. The implication of this assumption is that factor rewards are the same everywhere in the long run but not necessarily in the short run.†

3. The production function in the first industry contains a random variable and is of the form

$$X_1 = \alpha F_1(K_1, L_1) = \alpha L_1 f_1(k_1) \tag{2.1}$$

where the subscripts refer to the sectors, k is the capital/labour ratio, $\alpha f_1(k_1)$ is the average product of labour in X_1, and α is a random variable with a density function $g(\alpha)$ and a mean $E[\alpha] = \mu$. We assume that α is given in the probabilistic sense.‡

4. Producers in the first sector, who have to make production decisions prior to a knowledge of α, seek to maximise expected utility from profits and are risk-averse. Furthermore, all producers have the same utility function. The price of the first good is assumed to be the numeraire. Let π be the profit level in the first industry, and U be the utility attainable from it. Then expressed in terms of the first good,

$$\pi = X_1 - w_1 L_1 - r_1 K_1 \tag{2.2}$$

and

$$U = U(\pi)$$

where w_i is the real wage-rate, and r_i the real rental of capital in the ith sector. Taking the factor and commodity prices as given, the producers in the first industry then maximise $E[U] = E[U(\pi)]$. This yields the following relationships:§

$$E[U'(\alpha F_{L1} - w_1)] = 0 \tag{2.3}$$

$$E[U'(\alpha F_{K1} - r_1)] = 0 \tag{2.4}$$

where $\alpha F_{L1} = \alpha(f_1 - k_1 f_1')$ is the marginal product of labour, $\alpha F_{K1} = \alpha f_1'$ is the marginal product of capital,¶ and $f_1' =$

† If we assume perfect downward flexibility of factor prices, that is, factor owners accept lower remuneration rather than be unemployed, then it is legitimate to assume full employment of factors both in the short run and the long run. However, factor rewards need not be the same in both industries in the short run.

‡ In other words, X_1 producers have no say in the determination of the subjective probability distribution of α.

§ For a detailed derivation of these relationships, see Chapter 1.

¶ These are the properties of the linear homogeneous functions. For a detailed derivation, see Batra [1, chap. 1].

$df_1(k_1)/dk_1$. It may be noted here that risk-aversion on the part of producers implies that their utility functions are strictly concave, that is,

$$U'(\pi) > 0 \quad \text{and} \quad U''(\pi) < 0.$$

Equations (2.3) and (2.4) yield the following expressions for factor rewards:

$$w_1 = \frac{E[U'\alpha]}{E[U']} F_{L1} \tag{2.3*}$$

and

$$r_1 = \frac{E[U'\alpha]}{E[U']} F_{K1}. \tag{2.4*}$$

5. There is no uncertainty in the second industry, and producers there maximise utility from profits. The production function of the second industry is then given by

$$X_2 = L_2 f_2(k_2). \tag{2.5}$$

The utility-maximising conditions for producers in the second industry are

$$w_2 = p(f_2 - k_2 f_2') \tag{2.6}$$

and

$$r_2 = p f_2' \tag{2.7}$$

where p is the relative price of the second good in terms of the first.

Assumptions 1–5 may now be used to describe the production side of our model. With perfect competition in all markets and full factor mobility, factor rewards in the long run are the same everywhere, so that

$$w_1 = w_2 = w$$

and

$$r_1 = r_2 = r.$$

In view of this, (2.3*), (2.4*), (2.6) and (2.7) yield the following factor market equilibrium conditions:

$$(f_1 - k_1 f_1')E[U'\alpha] = p(f_2 - k_2 f_2')E[U'] \tag{2.8}$$

and

$$f_1' E[U'\alpha] = pf_2' E[U'].\qquad(2.9)$$

Under full employment

$$L_1 + L_2 = L\qquad(2.10)$$

and

$$L_1 k_1 + L_2 k_2 = K.\qquad(2.11)$$

This completes the description of the production side of our two-factor, two-good model where production in one sector is subject to random influences. The demand side will be introduced wherever necessary.

The structure of production in the economy is determined by six independent equations including (2.1), (2.5) and 2.8)–(2.11). If we treat p, K and L as parameters, then there are seven variables, X_1, X_2, k_1, k_2, L_1, L_2 and π. However, since in view of (2.6) and (2.7), π from (2.2) becomes

$$\begin{aligned}\pi &= X_1 - p(f_2 - k_2 f_2')L_1 - pf_2' K_1 \\ &= L_1[\alpha f_1 - p(f_2 - k_2 f_2') - pk_1 f_2']\end{aligned}\qquad(2.12)$$

so that with f_i and f_i' depending only on k_i, π is a function of L_1, p, k_1 and k_2. Hence, we have a determinate system of six independent equations, six unknowns and three parameters.

2.2 Development of the General Solution

We are now in a position to explore the salient features of the model developed above. We first obtain the general solutions, of which the particular cases will be examined in the subsequent sections.

In the absence of uncertainty, the simple way of solving the entire system is to obtain the solutions first for dk_1 and dk_2 from the two equations (2.8) and (2.9), second for dL_1 and dL_2 in terms of dk_1 and dk_2 from the two equations (2.10) and (2.11), and finally, for dX_1 and dX_2 from the two production functions. In the presence of uncertainty, however, the two equations (2.8) and (2.9) contain three variables k_1, k_2 and π, so that it is not possible to first solve for dk_1 and dk_2 in terms of a change in the parameters only. But the solutions for dk_1, dk_2, dL_1 and dL_2 can be obtained if we use the four equations (2.8)–(2.11), because π from (2.12) is related to L_1, k_1 and k_2. Further simplification can be achieved by using (2.10) and eliminating L_2 in (2.11) to obtain

$$L_1(k_1 - k_2) = K - k_2 L. \tag{2.13}$$

Differentiating the three equations (2.8), (2.9) and (2.13), and using (2.12), we obtain the following matrix, of which the detailed derivation is provided in the appendix (section 2.12):

$$
\begin{bmatrix}
A_1 & B_1 & C_1 \\
A_2 & B_2 & C_2 \\
(k_1 - k_2) & L_1 & L_2
\end{bmatrix}
\begin{bmatrix}
dL_1 \\
dk_1 \\
dk_2
\end{bmatrix}
=
\begin{bmatrix}
H_1 dp \\
H_2 dp \\
R
\end{bmatrix}
\tag{2.14}
$$

where, if we let $p = 1$ initially, and $\alpha F_{K1} - r = h_1 = (\alpha F_{L1} - w)/\omega$,

$$
\begin{aligned}
A_1/\omega = A_2 &= E[U'' h_1^2 (k_1 + \omega)] \\
B_1 &= E[\omega L_1 U'' h_1^2 - k_1 f_1'' U' \alpha] \\
B_2 &= E[L_1 U'' h_1^2 + f_1'' U' \alpha] \\
C_1 &= E[\omega L_1 f_2'' (k_2 - k_1) U'' h_1 + k_2 f_2'' U'] \\
C_2 &= E[L_1 f_2'' (k_2 - k_1) U'' h_1 - f_2'' U'] \\
H_1/\omega = H_2 &= f_2' E[L_1 (\omega + k_1) U'' h_1 + U']
\end{aligned}
\tag{2.15}
$$

and

$$R = dK - k_2 dL.$$

Let D be the denominator of the system (2.14). We show in the appendix that

$$
D =
\begin{vmatrix}
A_1 & B_1 & C_1 \\
A_2 & B_2 & C_2 \\
(k_1 - k_2) & L_1 & L_2
\end{vmatrix}
> 0.
\tag{2.16}
$$

The system (2.14) can be solved with the help of Cramer's Rule to obtain

$$dk_1 = \frac{C[(k_1 - k_2) H_2 dp - A_2 R]}{D}, \tag{2.17}$$

$$dk_2 = \frac{B[(k_1 - k_2) H_2 dp - A_2 R]}{D} \tag{2.18}$$

and

$$dL_1 = \frac{R(B_1 C_2 - B_2 C_1) - (L_2 B + L_1 C) H_2 dp}{D} \qquad (2.19)$$

where

$$B = B_1 - \omega B_2 = -f_1''(k_1 + \omega) E[U'\alpha] > 0 \qquad (2.20)$$

and

$$C = \omega C_2 - C_1 = -f_2''(k_2 + \omega) E[U'] > 0 \qquad (2.21)$$

because $f_i'' < 0, (i = 1, 2),$† and $E[U'\alpha]$ and $E[U']$ are both positive.

Equations (2.17)–(2.19) furnish the general solutions, which can be used to examine the specific properties of the two-sector model under uncertainty.

2.3 Factor Endowments and Factor Prices

In the certainty model, factor prices are not related to factor supplies as long as both goods are produced in the economy. The reason is that the real reward of each factor is governed by the product-price ratio as well as the marginal factor productivity, which in turn is determined only by the capital/labour ratio in each sector, thanks to the linear homogeneity of the production functions. Factor endowments play no role in this connection, so that, with given product prices, factor prices are unchanged.

We will now show that this result continues to hold under uncertainty if the firms in the first sector are risk-neutral, but not if they are risk-averse. Suppose that the product-price ratio is unaltered, so that $dp = 0$. Then, from (2.17), (2.18) and (2.15),

$$dk_1 = \frac{-CE[U''h_1^2](k_1 + \omega)(dK - k_2 dL)}{D} \qquad (2.22)$$

and

$$dk_2 = \frac{-BE[U''h_1^2](k_1 + \omega)(dK - k_2 dL)}{D}. \qquad (2.23)$$

Given our assumption of a linearly homogeneous and concave production function, $f_i'' < 0$, so that both B and C from (2.20) and (2.21) are positive. If the producers are indifferent to risk, then $U'' = 0$, so

---

† The negative sign of f_i'' implies diminishing returns to factor-proportions.

that (2.22) and (2.23) make it clear that dk_1 and dk_2 both reduce to zero. However, if the producers are risk-averse, then U'', and hence, $E[U''h_1^2]$ are negative, so that with $D > 0$, dk_i is positively related to K and negatively to L. In other words, an increase in the supply of capital, alone, results at constant commodity prices in a rise in the capital/labour ratio in each industry, and conversely. The implications are reversed if the expanding factor is labour.

It is now a simple matter to deduce that, because of diminishing returns to factor proportions, a rise in the supply of capital promotes a decline in the real reward of capital but a rise in the real wage-rate, and conversely, if the expanding factor is labour. This can also be seen clearly by differentiating (2.6) and (2.7), with $p = 1$ initially, to obtain

$$dw = -k_2 f_2'' dk_2 \quad \text{and} \quad dr = f_2'' dk_2$$

so that, in view of (2.23),

$$dw = \frac{k_2 f_2'' BE[U''h_1^2](k_1 + \omega)(dK - k_2 dL)}{D}$$

and

$$dr = -\frac{f_2'' BE[U''h_1^2](k_1 + \omega)(dK - k_2 dL)}{D}.$$

Evidently, with f_2'' and U'' negative and D positive,

$$dw > 0 \quad \text{and} \quad dr < 0 \quad \text{for} \quad dK > 0 \quad \text{and} \quad dL = 0$$

and

$$dw < 0 \quad \text{and} \quad dr > 0 \quad \text{for} \quad dL > 0 \quad \text{and} \quad dK = 0.$$

The following general theorem is then immediate:

Theorem 2.1. At constant product prices, an augmentation in the supply of any factor stimulates a decline in the real reward of that factor and a rise in the real reward of the other factor, provided the firms are risk-averters.†

What is the economic explanation for the fact that when product prices are kept constant, factor endowments affect factor rewards in

† Actually, the hypothesis of non-increasing absolute risk-aversion is also germane to this analysis, because, as shown in the appendix, this hypothesis is a sufficient condition for $D > 0$.

the case of risk-aversion but not in the case of risk-indifference? In all respects, the case of risk-neutrality has properties which are similar to those of the customary deterministic model. All that changes is that, instead of dealing with marginal factor productivity, we use the concept of the expected value of marginal factor productivity. As with the certainty model, therefore, factor rewards are not related to factor endowments even in the presence of uncertainty, provided that producers exhibit apathy towards risk.

All this becomes clear from an examination of (2.3*) and (2.4*) which reveal that factor rewards, with a given p, are determined by marginal factor productivities as well as the term $E[U'\alpha]/E[U']$ which, of course, reduces to μ in the risk-neutrality case; and since μ is given, factor endowments, as with the certainty case, play no role in determining the level of real factor rewards. Thus, under certainty conditions as well as risk-indifference, real factor rewards are influenced by the same set of forces.

In the risk-aversion case, however, the term $E[U'\alpha]/E[U']$ is not a constant but a function of profits in X_1. The level of profits in the first sector in turn is determined by factor rewards as well as the output of the first industry, which, as we discover in the next section, is related to factor supplies. Let us then proceed with the argument in two steps. First, as with the risk-neutrality case, suppose that factor prices stay the same when factor endowments expand. This results in a change in the output of X_1, as well as in π, because

$$\pi = \alpha F_1(K_1, L_1) - wL_1 - rK_1$$

so that with w and r unchanged,

$$d\pi = (\alpha F_{L1} - w)dL_1 + (\alpha F_{K1} - r)dK_1.$$

Now there is no reason to suggest that $\alpha F_{L1} = w$ and $\alpha F_{K1} = r$, and since, as we show in the subsequent section, dL_1 and dK_1 are non-zero in the presence of changes in factor supplies, $d\pi \neq 0$. Now a change in π gives rise to a change in $E[U'\alpha]/E[U']$, and in order for the balance to be maintained in the factor market equilibrium equations, (2.8) and (2.9), there must be a change in f_i', and hence, k_i; this eventually generates a shift in the real factor rewards.

Until now, our concern in this section has been with the implications of factor endowments for the real rewards of labour and capital. There still remains the case of expected profits in the first industry. In the certainty case, long-run profits in a competitive model are zero, so that the question of the impact of factor supplies on profits does not arise. Expected profits also are zero in the presence of uncertainty, provided that producers are apathetic to risk. In the risk-aversion case, however, expected profits are positive. A little manipulation of (2.12) makes it amply clear. Suppose $\omega = w/r$ is the wage/rental ratio. Then, from (2.3*), (2.4*), (2.6) and (2.7),

$$\omega = \frac{F_{Li}}{F_{Ki}} = \frac{f_i - k_i f_i'}{f_i'}. \tag{2.24}$$

Using this in (2.12), we obtain

$$\pi = L_1[\alpha f_1 - p(f_2 - k_2 f_2') - pk_1 f_2']$$
$$= L_1(k_1 + \omega)(\alpha f_1' - r) \tag{2.25}$$

so that

$$E[\pi] = L_1[\mu f_1 - p(f_2 - k_2 f_2') - pk_1 f_2'] \tag{2.26}$$
$$= L_1(k_1 + \omega)(\mu f_1' - r) \tag{2.27}$$

is positive because $\mu f_1' \geqslant r$ when producers are risk-averse.†

Let us then explore the ramifications of factor endowments for expected profits with product prices unaltered. Differentiating (2.26) totally, writing $\bar{\pi}$ for $E[\pi]$, using (2.27) and remembering that p equals unity initially, we obtain

$$d\bar{\pi} = L_1[\bar{h}_1 dk_1 + f_2''(k_2 - k_1)dk_2] + \bar{h}_1(k_1 + \omega)dL_1$$

where $\bar{h}_1 = \mu f_1' - r$. Substituting for dk_1, dk_2 and dL_1 from (2.17)–(2.19), we obtain

$$d\bar{\pi} = -\frac{R[L_1\bar{h}_1 CA_2 + L_1 f_2''(k_2 - k_1)BA_2 - \bar{h}_1(k_1 + \omega)(B_1C_2 - B_2C_1)]}{D}.$$

Since by adding and subtracting $B_1 C_1/\omega$, we can write

$$B_1 C_2 - B_2 C_1 = \frac{B_1(\omega C_2 - C_1)}{\omega} + \frac{C_1(B_1 - \omega B_2)}{\omega} = \frac{B_1 C}{\omega} + \frac{C_1 B}{\omega},$$

---

† This was established in Chapter 1, where we concluded that a risk-averse firm hires inputs in such a way that input prices fall short of the value of the expected marginal factor productivities.

$$d\bar{\pi} =$$

$$-\frac{R\left[\left(L_1 A_2 - B_1 \frac{k_1+\omega}{\omega}\right)\bar{h}_1 C + L_1 f_2''(k_2 - k_1)A_2 B - \bar{h}_1(k_1+\omega)\frac{C_1}{\omega}B\right]}{D}.$$

Substituting for B and C from (2.20) and (2.21), for A_2, B_1 and C_1 from (2.15), and remembering that now h_1 is replaced by $\bar{h}_1$ and α by μ, the expression for $d\bar{\pi}$ becomes

$$d\bar{\pi} = \frac{\mu \bar{h}_1 (k_1+\omega)E[U']^2 f_1'' f_2''(k_1 - k_2)R}{D}. \tag{2.28}$$

Suppose only capital is growing, so that $R = dK$. Then, since $D > 0$, $f_i'' < 0$ and $\bar{h}_1 > 0$, we conclude from (2.27) that an increase in the supply of capital raises expected profits in the first sector provided the first sector is capital-intensive relative to the second, and conversely. The following general theorem can now be derived:

Theorem 2.2. An increase in the supply of any factor at constant commodity prices promotes an increase in the expected profit level in X_1 if the first sector is intensive in the use of the expanding factor, and conversely.

2.4 Factor Endowments and Outputs

In this section, we explore the implications of changes in factor supplies for the outputs in the two sectors, given that commodity prices are constant. Working with the deterministic two-sector model, Rybczynski [4] has shown that, at constant commodity prices, an increase in the supply of any factor augments the production of the commodity which is intensive in the use of the expanding factor and lowers the output of the good which is unintensive in the use of that factor. The logic behind the Rybczynski theorem is very simple.

Consider the following expression for the overall capital/labour ratio in the economy:

$$k = \frac{K}{L} = \frac{K_1}{L_1} \cdot \frac{L_1}{L} + \frac{K_2}{L_2} \cdot \frac{L_2}{L}$$

$$= k_1 \frac{L_1}{L} + k_2 \frac{L_2}{L}.$$

This expression states that the overall K/L ratio is a weighted average of the capital/labour ratios in the two sectors. Suppose there occurs an increase in the supply of capital alone, so that K rises. As stated before, k_1 and k_2 remain unchanged in the certainty model if commodity prices are kept constant. This means that an increase in k must be matched by changes in L_1/L and L_2/L. Now if X_1 is capital-intensive, it is clear that L_1/L must rise, so that $(L_2/L) = 1 - (L_1/L)$ must decline. A close inspection of the production functions given by (2.1) and (2.5) reveals that these changes will lead to an increase in X_1 and a decline in X_2. This is the argument inherent in the Rybczynski theorem.

Does the Rybczynski theorem hold in the model where production occurs in a stochastic environment? The answer is a definite Yes, in spite of the fact that factor proportions in the two industries are now affected by changes in factor supplies, provided the absolute risk-aversion of producers in the first industry is non-increasing in profits.

Since output in the first industry is random, it makes little sense to speak in terms of a change in the output of X_1. However, the problem can be formulated in terms of two equivalent ways. First, one could investigate the effects of various levels of K and L for the expected output of X_1 and the output of X_2 at any given p. Second, one may be interested in the actual output of X_1 for any p at varying levels of K and L, because if $E[X_1]$ for any p is different at different levels of K and L, so would be the actual output of X_1 obtained after the actual value of α becomes known. Suppose α^* is the actual value of α. In general, α^* is different from $E[\alpha]$, but this makes little difference to the question under discussion. In the present section, we examine the impact of changes in factor supplies on X_2 and $E[X_1]$ at constant commodity prices, whereas in the next chapter we shall utilise the relationship between factor endowments and the actual output of X_1.

The expected output of the first good is given by

$$\overline{X}_1 = \mu L_1 f_1(k_1). \tag{2.29}$$

In order to obtain the effect of a change, say, in the supply of capital on $\overline{X}_1$, differentiate (2.29) with respect to K to obtain

$$\frac{\partial \overline{X}_1}{\partial K} = \mu \left[L_1 f_1' \frac{\partial k_1}{\partial K} + f_1 \frac{\partial L_1}{\partial K} \right].$$

Remembering that now $dp = dL = 0$, and $R = dK$, and substituting from (2.17) and (2.19), we obtain

$$\frac{\partial \overline{X}_1}{\partial K} = \frac{\mu[-L_1 f_1' C A_2 + f_1(B_1 C_2 - B_2 C_1)]}{D}. \tag{2.30}$$

Substituting from (2.15) and (2.21) in (2.30) then yields

$$\frac{\partial \overline{X}_1}{\partial K} = \frac{\mu f_1 f_1'' f_2'' \{L_1(k_1+\omega)E[U''h_1]+E[U']\}E[U'\alpha](k_1-k_2)}{D}. \tag{2.31}$$

In the same manner, we can obtain

$$\frac{\partial X_2}{\partial K} = L_2 f_2' \frac{\partial k_2}{\partial K} + f_2 \frac{\partial L_2}{\partial K}$$

$$= -\frac{f_2 f_1'' f_2'' \{L_1(k_1+\omega)E[U''h_1]+E[U']\}E[U'\alpha](k_1-k_2)}{D}. \tag{2.32}$$

Consider first the case where firms are risk-neutral, so that $U'' = 0$. Since $f_1'' f_2'' > 0$, and D is positive, it is clear from (2.31) and (2.32) that

$$\frac{\partial \overline{X}_1}{\partial k} \gtrless 0 \quad \text{if} \quad k_1 \gtrless k_2 \tag{2.33}$$

and

$$\frac{\partial X_2}{\partial K} \gtrless 0 \quad \text{if} \quad k_2 \gtrless k_1. \tag{2.34}$$

In other words, the Rybczynski theorem holds unambiguously.

In the presence of risk-averse behaviour, however, $U'' < 0$, and in order to interpret equations (2.31) and (2.32), we also need the sign of $E[U''h_1]$. In the appendix, we demonstrate that $E[U''h_1] \geqslant 0$ in the presence of non-increasing absolute risk-aversion. With $E[U''h_1] \geqslant 0$, it is clear from a close inspection of (2.31) and (2.32) that the sign of $\partial \overline{X}_1/\partial K$ and $\partial X_2/\partial K$ are governed, as in the risk-neutral case, solely by the sign of $(k_1 - k_2)$. This means that the expressions (2.33) and (2.34) and hence the Rybczynski theorem continue to be valid, if the absolute risk-aversion is non-increasing in profits. The implications of an increase in the supply of labour alone for the two outputs can be derived analogously. The following theorem is immediate:

Theorem 2.3. Non-increasing absolute risk-aversion of producers is sufficient to ensure the validity of the Rybczynski theorem.

2.5   Factor and Commodity Prices

In the deterministic two-sector model, Samuelson [5] has shown that when both goods are produced in any economy, then there exists a one-to-one relationship between the factor-price ratio and the commodity-price ratio; furthermore, the factor-price ratio is not affected by factor supplies. In our uncertainty model, we have already shown that the latter result does not hold, but it turns out that the former result continues to be valid in the presence of non-increasing absolute risk-aversion. In what follows, we assume that factor supplies are constant, so that $dK = dL = R = 0$.

From (2.24), the wage/rental ratio is given by

$$\omega = \frac{f_1 - k_1 f_1'}{f_1'}$$

so that

$$\frac{\partial \omega}{\partial p} = -\frac{f_1 f_1''}{f_1'^2} \cdot \frac{\partial k_1}{\partial p}.$$

Substituting from (2.17) then yields

$$\frac{\partial \omega}{\partial p} = -\frac{f_1 f_1'' C(k_1 - k_2) H_2}{f_1'^2 D} \tag{2.35}$$

where, from (2.15),

$$H_2 = f_2' E[L_1(\omega + k_1) U'' h_1 + U'].$$

With non-increasing absolute risk-aversion, $E[U'' h_1] \geqslant 0$, so that $H_2 > 0$. Since from (2.21), $C > 0$, and since $f_1'' < 0$ and $D > 0$, it is clear that the sign of $\partial \omega / \partial p$ is the same as the sign of $(k_1 - k_2)$. Thus, given that $k_1 \neq k_2$, (2.35) defines a unique relationship between ω and p. Specifically, an increase in p stimulates a rise in the wage/rental ratio if the first sector is capital-intensive relative to the second, and vice versa.

The significance of non-reversible factor intensities in the uniqueness of the relation between p and ω also comes out clearly from (2.35), because if $k_1 > k_2$ for some levels of ω, and $k_1 < k_2$ for other levels, then p and ω will be positively related for some range of ω, and negatively for some other. It is then possible that some level of p may be associated with multiple values of ω.

2.6 The Price–Output Response

This section is concerned with the investigation of the effects of a change in the commodity-price ratio on the expected output of X_1 and the output of X_2. In the certainty case, commodity prices and the outputs are positively related, that is, the supply curve of each good is positively sloped. This result continues to hold under uncertainty, provided absolute risk-aversion is non-increasing in profits.

Since production decisions in the first industry are made prior to the resolution of the random variable α, a change in the commodity-price ratio, p, does not induce any change in the two outputs in the short run where factors, once employed in any sector, remain there until the time comes for the next decision-making by the X_1 producers. At the time of decision-making, X_1 producers, of course, respond to the new level of p by utilising inputs in smaller or larger amounts than before. As a result, some factors must move from one sector to the other. Thus, in the short run, outputs do not respond to changes in commodity prices, but in the long run they do. What is then the nature of this response, given that factor supplies are constant?

As before, the expected output of X_1 is given by

$$\overline{X}_1 = \mu L_1 f_1(k_1).$$

Differentiating this with respect to p, we obtain

$$\frac{\partial \overline{X}_1}{\partial p} = \mu \left[L_1 f_1' \frac{\partial k_1}{\partial p} + f_1 \frac{\partial L_1}{\partial p} \right]$$

which, after substitution from (2.17) and (2.19) and the use of the definition of ω, becomes

$$\frac{\partial \overline{X}_1}{\partial p} = -\frac{\mu[L_1 C(\omega + k_2) f_1' + L_2 f_1 B] H_2}{D}.$$

In the same way we can obtain

$$\frac{\partial X_2}{\partial p} = \frac{[L_2 B(\omega + k_1) f_2' + L_1 f_2 C] H_2}{D}.$$

It is clear that non-increasing absolute risk-aversion of X_1 producers, which, as shown before, ensures the positive sign of H_2, is sufficient for $\partial \overline{X}_1 / \partial p < 0$ and $\partial X_2 / \partial p > 0$. In other words, an increase in the relative price of the second good leads, in the long run, to a decline in $\overline{X}_1$ and a rise in X_2, and conversely; in other words, the supply curves for the two goods are positively inclined, provided, of course, that the absolute risk-aversion is non-increasing.

2.7   The Expected Transformation Curve

For several decades, the transformation curve has played a very significant role in facilitating the exposition of various problems arising in the theory of international trade. A similar tool of analysis needs to be developed to enable us to examine some issues arising in the realm of the probabilistic theory of international trade. Accordingly, corresponding to the certainty concept of the transformation curve, we introduce the uncertainty counterpart, the expected transformation curve. The difference between the two concepts is merely the fact that in the certainty case, the transformation curve is a locus of the 'efficient' outputs of the two goods, whereas the expected transformation curve is defined by the locus of efficient expected outputs of X_1 and the outputs of X_2, with production efficiency in both cases being defined in the sense of the Pareto optimality criterion, which suggests that a combination of two outputs is efficient if every other feasible reallocation of inputs diminishes the output of at least one commodity. In every other respect, the two concepts are alike. Thus, the expected transformation curve, like the certainty counterpart, has a negative slope and is concave towards the origin. The reasons for this concavity in the stochastic model are the same as those for the deterministic model. In both cases, commodity and factor markets are perfect, supply curves are positively sloped, and there are no intersectoral factor-price differentials.†

What is the slope of the expected transformation curve in equilibrium? Here, the result is markedly different from that available in the certainty case where the marginal rate of transformation in equilibrium reflects the commodity- price ratio. In the uncertainty case, however, it turns out that this latter result no longer holds. This is demonstrated below.

As before, the expected output of the first industry is

$$\overline{X}_1 = \mu F_1(K_1, L_1)$$

---

† The absence of inter-industry factor-price differentials is important, because several economists have recently shown that in the presence of such differentials, the transformation curve may become convex to the origin in spite of the positively sloped supply curves. For a survey of this type of literature, see Magee [3] and Batra [1. chap. 10].

whereas

$$X_2 = F_2(K_2, L_2).$$

Differentiating these totally, and dividing $d\overline{X}_1$ by dX_2, we obtain

$$\frac{d\overline{X}_1}{dX_2} = \frac{\mu(F_{K1}dK_1 + F_{L1}dL_1)}{F_{K2}dK_2 + F_{L2}dL_2}.$$

Using the factor market equilibrium conditions (2.8) and (2.9) and, from the full-employment conditions, the fact that $dK_1 = -dK_2$ and $dL_1 = -dL_2$, we obtain

$$\frac{d\overline{X}_1}{dX_2} = -\frac{p(F_{K2}dK_2 + F_{L2}dL_2)E[U']\mu}{(F_{K2}dK_2 + F_{L2}dL_2)E[U'\alpha]}$$

$$= -\frac{p\mu E[U']}{E[U'\alpha]}. \tag{2.36*}$$

Noting that the expected value of the product of two terms equals the product of their expected values plus their covariance,[†] that is,

$$E[U'\alpha] = \mu E[U'] + \operatorname{cov}(U', \alpha)$$

and substituting this in (2.36*), we get

$$\frac{d\overline{X}_1}{dX_2} = -\frac{p\mu E[U']}{\mu E[U'] + \operatorname{cov}(U', \alpha)} = -\beta p \tag{2.36}$$

where

$$\beta = \frac{\mu E[U']}{\mu E[U'] + \operatorname{cov}(U', \alpha)} \tag{2.37}$$

If the covariance is zero, so that the firms are apathetic to risk, $d\overline{X}_1/dX_2$ or the marginal rate of expected transformation equals the negative of the commodity-price ratio, because then $\beta = 1$. However, with risk-averse firms, the covariance, as established in the preceding chapter, is negative so that $\beta > 1$. Thus, with risk-aversion,

$$-\frac{d\overline{X}_1}{dX_2} > p.$$

The results derived in this section are further clarified by examination of Fig. 2.1, where TT' is the expected transformation curve

† See Chapter 1 for details.

which is concave to the origin; AB is the price line whose slope reflects the commodity-price ratio, p, which the competitive producers take as given. In the risk-indifference case, the production point is given by P where AB touches TT' so that the slopes of AB and TT' are identical or, what amounts to the same thing, the marginal rate of expected transformation equals $-p$. However, in the risk-aversion case, the production point will lie on TT' between T' and P, because only then will $-d\bar{X}_1/dX_2$ be greater than p. Suppose the production point with risk-averse behaviour is given by P', where

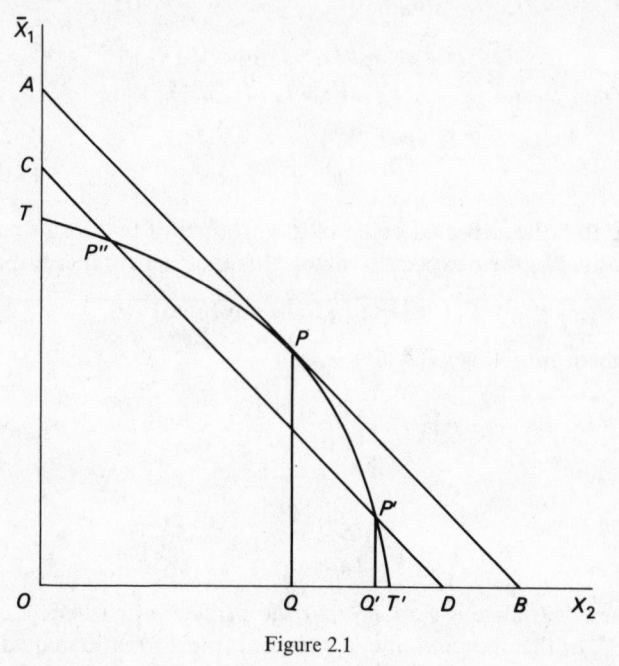

Figure 2.1

the absolute value of the marginal rate of expected transformation is greater than p, which is displayed by the slope of CD parallel to AB. At P', $\bar{X}_1$ equals $P'Q'$, and X_2 equals OQ'. The comparison of these with the point P, where $\bar{X}_1 = PQ$ and $X_2 = OQ$, reveals that with risk-aversion, the expected output of X_1 is smaller, and the output of X_2 larger than those available in the risk-neutrality case.

It is a simple matter now to conclude that this result is reversed in the case of risk-preference, which will yield a production point such as P''.

Until now, our concern has been with the properties of the expected transformation curve. The exposition of some problems appearing in the subsequent chapters, however, can be better handled by the concept of the 'actual' transformation curve, which may be defined as the locus of efficient actual outputs of the two goods. If α^* is the realised value of α, then the actual output of X_1 is given by

$$X_1^* = \alpha^* F_1(K_1, L_1) = \alpha^* L_1 f_1(k).$$ (2.38)

The actual transformation curve then is a locus of the efficient levels of X_1^* and X_2.

Since the decision-making by X_1 producers is done before knowledge of α^*, the properties of the actual and the expected transformation curves are the same, except that now

$$\frac{dX_1^*}{dX_2} = -\frac{\alpha^* E[U']}{\mu E[U'] + \text{cov}(U', \alpha)} p = -\beta^* p$$ (2.39)

and it is no longer certain that β^*, unlike β, is greater than unity.† For α^* may be greater than, less than, or the same as μ. Whenever we use the concept of the actual transformation curve in subsequent chapters, this latter qualification will be relevant.

2.8 The Stolper–Samuelson Theorem

According to the Stolper–Samuelson theorem [6], an increase in the relative price of any good stimulates an increase in the real reward of the factor used intensively by that good and a decline in the real reward of the other factor. We will now demonstrate that this theorem continues to be valid in the presence of uncertainty, provided the absolute risk-aversion is non-increasing.

The economic explanation of our result is this. From (2.17) and (2.18), it is clear that with $D > 0$, $R = 0$, and with $H_2 > 0$ because of non-increasing absolute risk-aversion, an increase in the relative price of the second good results in a rise in the capital/labour ratio in both sectors if the first sector is capital-intensive relative to the second, and conversely, if the first sector is the relatively labour-intensive sector. As a result, the marginal product of capital declines (rises) and that of labour rises (declines) if $k_1 > k_2$ (if $k_1 < k_2$) in both sectors. Since the real reward of each factor is determined by

---

† Equation (2.39) can be derived in the same manner as (2.36).

its marginal productivity in sector 2, a rise in p leads to a rise in the real reward of labour and a decline in the real reward of capital if $k_1 > k_2$, and conversely, if $k_1 < k_2$. This readily establishes the Stolper–Samuelson theorem in our uncertainty framework, but the key to the proof lies in the unambiguous sign of H_2, which is unequivocally positive only under non-increasing absolute risk-aversion of producers.

A diagrammatic illustration of this result is provided by Fig. 2.2 which portrays the Edgeworth–Bowley box diagram, where the expected output of X_1 and the output of X_2 are respectively measured

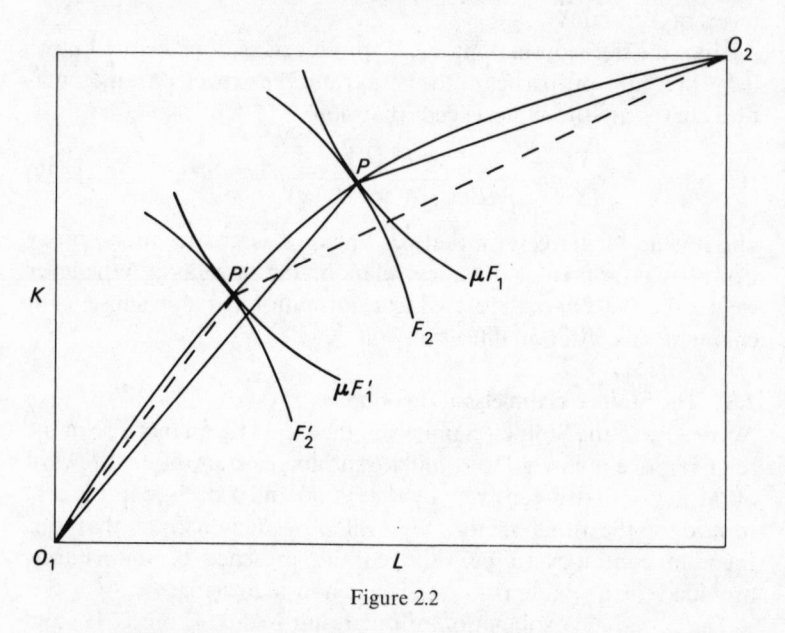

Figure 2.2

with reference to the origins O_1 and O_2. The expected output of the first good increases as the $\overline{X}_1$ isoquants such as $\mu F_1'$ and μF_1 move away from O_1, whereas the output of X_2 increases if the X_2 isoquants such as F_2 and F_2' move away from O_2. The given supplies of capital and labour are measured respectively along the vertical and the horizontal axes. Each point in the box represents a certain allocation of the two inputs between the two sectors. However, efficient points of production are those which are defined by the tangency of the various isoquants of the two goods. The locus of these efficient production points may be called the expected contract curve, whose location in the box reflects the fact that X_1 is capital-intensive relative to X_2. Since w and r are the same in both sectors, and since in each sector the wage/rental ratio equals the ratio of marginal products, the marginal rates of factor substitution in equilibrium are also the same between the two sectors. Hence, in spite of the risk-averse behaviour in X_1, the production point lies on the expected contract curve.

The selection of the production point on the expected contract curve is determined by the commodity-price ratio. Suppose the initial production point is given by P. If there is an increase in the relative price of the second good, then we know from section 2.6 that under non-increasing absolute risk-aversion, X_2 rises and the expected output of X_1 declines, so that the production point moves from P to P'. Prior to the increase in p, the capital/labour ratio in the two industries is given by the slopes of the rays O_1P and O_2P, whereas after the rise in p, the capital/labour ratios in the two sectors rise to those given by the slopes of O_1P' and O_2P'. Once this is established, the Stolper–Samuelson theorem follows immediately.

2.9 The Closed-Economy Equilibrium

Until now, our concern has been with the properties of the production structure of the two-sector economy. In exploring these properties, we have assumed that competitive producers take commodity prices as given. But what in the economy determines the commodity prices?

In an economy consisting of competitive markets, product prices are determined by the forces of demand and supply, and if the economy is not exposed to international trade, then in the autarky equilibrium domestic demand and supply must be equal for each commodity. What then is the nature of the closed-economy equilibrium? The answer to this question determines the way that the commodity-price ratio is determined in our model.

If we assume that, behaving like a rational individual, the community seeks to maximise total satisfaction from the consumption of the two goods, the problem can be formulated as one of maximising an aggregate utility function subject to the constraint imposed by the available factor supplies – a constraint inherent in the construction of the transformation curve, which describes that $X_1 = X_1(X_2)$. It is important to remember that to determine the commodity-price ratio, the actual output of each good is to be equated to its demand. Thus, even though production decisions in the first industry are made prior to knowledge of the random variable α, the commodity-price ratio in the economy is determined only after the actual value of α becomes known and markets get cleared.

For the sake of exposition, let us assume for the time being that the actual value of α equals its expected value μ, so that the actual and the expected transformation curves are identical to TT' in Fig.

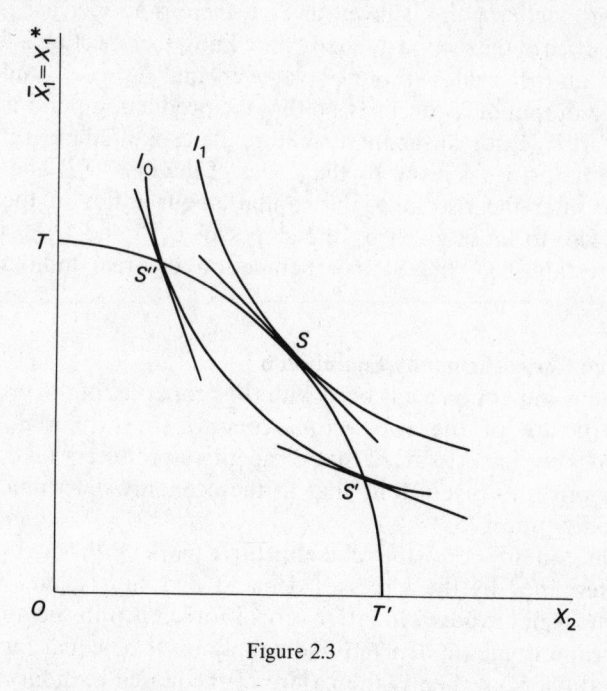

Figure 2.3

2.3. A closed economy can produce and consume along any point on TT'; community welfare, however, is maximised at point S, where the community indifference curve I_1 is tangential to the transformation curve. The commodity-price ratio is given by the slope of the common tangent drawn through S.

Point S, however, is available to the economy only if the producers in the first industry are risk-indifferent, because only then is the marginal rate of expected transformation equal to the negative of the commodity-price ratio. In the case of risk-aversion, the closed-economy equilibrium will be given by any point between T' and S because, now, the absolute value of the marginal rate of expected transformation exceeds the commodity-price ratio; S' is one such point where the relative price of the second good is given by the tangent to the community indifference curve I_0 at S'. By contrast, if X_1 producers are risk-preferers, then equilibrium is at a point like S'' and the autarky commodity-price ratio is given by the slope of the tangent to I_0 drawn through S''.

Until now, we have assumed that $\alpha^* = \mu$, that is, the actual value of α is the same as its expected value. In general, this assumption is not likely to be satisfied, in which case the actual commodity-price ratio is determined in a manner different from that depicted in Fig. 2.3. It is useful in this connection to introduce a distinction between the actual and the expected commodity-price ratio. Let $\bar{p}$ be the commodity-price ratio that would equate the output of X_2 and the expected output of X_1 to the respective demands for the two goods. We call $\bar{p}$ the expected commodity-price ratio. Now $\bar{p}$ would be the same as the actual product-price ratio, p, only if $\alpha^* = \mu$. Obviously, if $\alpha^* \neq \mu$, $p \neq \bar{p}$.

We will now show that if $\alpha^* > \mu$, then $p > \bar{p}$ and for $\alpha^* < \mu$, $p < \bar{p}$. This result is valid regardless of the risk-attitude of the X_1 producers. However, in what follows we will concentrate on the risk-averse behaviour.

Consider Fig. 2.4 where, as before, TT' is the expected transformation curve, S' is the autarky equilibrium point if $\alpha^* = \mu$ and if, of course, X_1 producers are risk-averse, $\bar{p}$ is displayed by the slope of the tangent AB, the output of X_2 equals OQ, and the expected output of X_1 is furnished by $S'Q$.

Consider now the case where $\alpha^* > \mu$, so that $X_1^* > \bar{X}_1$, and since X_2 is not affected by the realised level of α, the actual production point is given by, say, G; the market-clearing-price ratio is then given by the slope of the indifference curve I_2 at point G. Since CD is steeper than AB, $p > \bar{p}$.

On the other hand, if $\alpha^* < \mu$, the production point is given by a point such as H, and the market-clearing-price ratio is reflected by the slope of EF, which is less steep than AB, so that $p < \bar{p}$.

2.10 The Case of Joint-Product Firms

It has been suggested by some economists that a risk-averse individual faced with an uncertain economic environment and a choice to invest in certain, as well as uncertain prospects usually chooses investments with safe returns or diversifies his portfolio by investing in both risky and certain prospects. Similarly, risk-averse firms diversify by producing goods in risky, as well as non-risky markets. In terms of our two-sector model where uncertainty is present only in the production of one good, the diversification hypothesis implies that risk-averse firms will either produce the second good where there is no uncertainty or they will produce

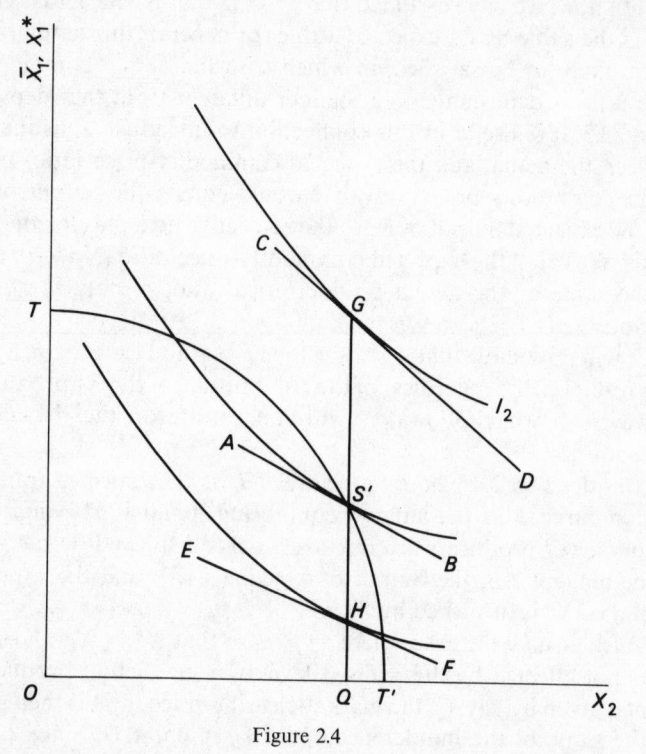

Figure 2.4

both goods. Does this make any difference to our analysis, which has so far been based on the assumption that firms are single-product and not joint-product firms?

It turns out that our analysis remains unmodified even if some firms are involved with the production of both goods. The reason is that most of our results depend on the factor market equilibrium conditions furnished by (2.8) and (2.9), and these conditions remain unchanged regardless of whether the firms are single- or joint-product firms. We can safely postulate that there are some firms which produce only the second good and, while maximising utility from profits, they hire inputs in such a way that the price of each factor equals the value of its marginal product. Given our assumptions of perfect markets and linearly homogeneous production functions, total revenue equals total cost, and in the long-run equilibrium, X_2 producers make zero profits.

Since factors are fully mobile in the long run, all firms face the same factor prices. Now if the producers engaged in the production of the first good are single-product producers, then, of course, their expected utility-maximising behaviour will yield the two first-order conditions (2.3) and (2.4). However, if the X_1 producers also produce X_2, the first-order conditions for expected utility maximisation stay the same. In producing X_1, the producers will set w and r to the expressions contained in (2.3*) and (2.4*), whereas in producing X_2, the same set of producers will, in accordance with (2.6) and (2.7), respectively, equate w and r with the marginal value productivity of labour and capital. For, if these joint-product firms do not follow the behaviour represented by (2.6) and (2.7), they will be suffering losses, because the most they can earn in the long run from X_2 production is zero profit.† Furthermore, since they make no profit from X_2 production, their utility from profits in the first sector is unchanged, irrespective of whether they are joint- or single-product producers. Thus, we see that all our first-order conditions presented in section 2.2 remain unmodified. It follows, then, that the factor market equilibrium conditions (2.8) and (2.9) also remain unaltered. Thus, it makes little difference to our analysis whether firms are single- or joint-product producers.‡

2.11 Summary
The preceding sections of this chapter have laid the foundation of a

---

† By profits, we mean the excess of total revenue over total costs, where the 'normal' return of the factor owners is included in the total cost of production. By making zero long-run profits, the competitive producers maximise the normal return on their supplies of capital and labour. On the other hand, if factor prices are not equated to the marginal value products of the inputs, the producers, operating under certainty conditions, will not be maximising the normal rate of return on their input supplies. Utility maximisation, however, rules out this behaviour.

‡ Actually, these arguments suggest that the factor market equilibrium conditions will be unchanged even if *all* firms are joint-product firms.

two-sector, two-factor, general equilibrium model, where production in one sector occurs under conditions of uncertainty. We discovered that most of the properties of the deterministic two-sector model carry over to our stochastic framework, provided absolute risk-aversion of the firms is a non-increasing function of their profits. Under this assumption and those which are usually maintained in the exposition of the traditional two-sector model, we were able to demonstrate that (1) the supply curves for both goods are positively sloped, (2) an increase in the relative price of any good results in a rise in the real reward of its intensive factor and a decline in the real reward of the other factor, and (3) an increase in the supply of any factor at constant commodity prices stimulates the expansion of the good using the expanding factor intensively at the expense of the output of the other good. In other words, the Stolper–Samuelson and the Rybczynski theorems were shown to be valid in our stochastic framework.

One result which is derivable from our model, and not the deterministic framework, concerns the implications of changes in factor supplies at constant commodity prices for the real reward of the two factors. In the certainty milieu, factor supplies play no role in determining factor rewards, so long as both goods are produced in the economy. However, in the stochastic model, an increase in the supply of any factor contributes to a decline in its real reward and a rise in the real reward of the other factor.

Another result which is typical of the probabilistic framework is that the marginal rate of expected transformation does not equal the negative of the commodity-price ratio, although the expected transformation curve itself continues to be concave towards the origin.

2.12   Appendix

There are three tasks assigned to this appendix. First, we will explicitly derive the equations contained in the system (2.14) presented in the text. A clear understanding of the derivations of this system is crucial to gain full insight into the working of our uncertainty model. Second, we will show that the denominator of the system (2.14), D, is positive. Finally, the sign of

$$E[U''h_1] = E[U''(\alpha F_{K1} - r)]$$

will be shown to be non-negative under the hypothesis of non-increasing absolute risk-aversion.

The two equations that underlie the derivation of the first equation of the system (2.14) are equations (2.8) and (2.12), which are

$$(f_1 - k_1 f_1')E[U'(\pi)\alpha] = p(f_2 - k_2 f_2')E[U'(\pi)] \qquad \text{(A.1)}$$

and

$$\pi = L_1[\alpha f_1 - p(f_2 - k_2 f_2') - pk_1 f_2']. \qquad \text{(A.2)}$$

It is worth noting here that with linearly homogeneous production functions, f_i and f_i' are functions only of k_i.

Differentiating (A.1) totally, we have

$$E[\alpha F_{L1} U'' d\pi - U'\alpha k_1 f_1'' dk_1] = pF_{L2}E[U'' d\pi] - pk_2 f_2'' dk_2 E[U']$$
$$+ F_{L2}E[U']dp \qquad \text{(A.3)}$$

where $U' \equiv U'(\pi)$, $F_{Li} \equiv f_i - k_i f_i'$, and so on. Note that from (2.6), $pF_{L2} = w$. Therefore, subtracting $wE[U'' d\pi]$ from both sides of (A.3) and remembering that initially $p = 1$, we get

$$E[(\alpha F_{L1} - w)U'' d\pi - U'\alpha k_1 f_1'' dk_1] = -k_2 f_2'' dk_2 E[U']$$
$$+ F_{L2}E[U']dp. \qquad \text{(A.4)}$$

Differentiating (A.2) totally and remembering that from (2.7), $pf_2' = r$, we obtain

$$d\pi = L_1[(\alpha F_{K1} - r)dk_1 + f_2''(k_2 - k_1)dk_2 - f_2'(k_1 + \omega)dp]$$
$$+ (\alpha F_{K1} - r)(k_1 + \omega)dL_1. \qquad \text{(A.5)}$$

In obtaining (A.5), we have made use of the fact that

$$\omega = \frac{f_i - k_i f_i'}{f_i'}$$

so that, from (A.2),

$$\pi = L_1[\alpha f_1'(\omega + k_1) - f_2'(\omega + k_1)p]$$
$$= L_1(\alpha F_{K1} - r)(\omega + k_1)$$

because $f_i' \equiv F_{Ki}$.

---

† This follows from the fact that

$$\omega = \frac{F_{Li}}{F_{Ki}}.$$

Substituting for $d\pi$ from (A.5) in (A.3), collecting terms and remembering that $(\alpha F_{L1} - w) = \omega(\alpha F_{K1} - r)$,† we obtain

$$E[U''(\alpha F_{K1} - r)^2(k_1 + \omega)]dL_1 + E[U''(\alpha F_{K1} - r)^2\omega L_1$$
$$- k_1 f_1'' U'\alpha]dk_1 + E[\omega L_1 f_2''(k_2 - k_1)U''(\alpha F_{K1} - r) + k_2 f_2'' U']dk_2$$
$$= E[L_1(k_1 + \omega)U''(\alpha F_{K1} - r) + U']\omega f_2' dp. \qquad (A.6)$$

This is the first equation of the system (2.14) in the text. Similarly, by differentiating (2.9) totally and utilising (A.5), we can obtain the second equation of (2.14).

We now turn to the sign of D. From (2.16)

$$D = L_1 A_2(C_1 - \omega C_2) + L_2 A_2(\omega B_2 - B_1) + (k_1 - k_2)(C_2 B_1 - C_1 B_2).$$
$$(A.7)$$

Substituting from (2.20) and (2.21) in (A.7), the first two terms of (A.7) become

$$(k_1 + \omega)E[U''h_1^2]\{L_1 f_2''(k_2 + \omega)E[U'] + L_2 f_1''(k_1 + \omega)E[U'\alpha]\}$$
$$(A.8)$$

whereas substituting from (2.15), the last term of (A.7) becomes

$$(k_1 + \omega)L_1 f_1'' f_2''(k_1 - k_2)^2 E[U'\alpha]E[U''h_1]$$
$$+ f_1'' f_2''(k_1 - k_2)^2 E[U']E[U'\alpha]$$
$$+ L_1 f_2''(k_2 + \omega)E[U']E[U''h_1^2](k_2 - k_1). \quad (A.9)$$

With $U'' < 0$ and $f_i'' < 0$, the expression in (A.8) is positive. Similarly, with $E[U''h_1] \geqslant 0$ under non-increasing absolute risk-aversion, the first term of (A.9) is positive and so is its second term, whereas its third term may be of any sign, depending on the sign of $(k_2 - k_1)$. But if we combine the first term of (A.8) with the last term of (A.9), we get

$$L_1 f_2''(k_2 + \omega)^2 E[U']E[U''h_1^2]$$

which is clearly positive. Hence D is positive. Note that non-increasing absolute risk-aversion is sufficient but not necessary for $D > 0$.

Let us now investigate the sign of

$$E[U''h_1] = E[U''(\alpha F_{K1} - r)].$$

As defined in the previous chapter, the index of absolute risk-aversion is given by

$$R_a(\pi) = -\frac{U''(\pi)}{U'(\pi)}. \qquad \text{(A.10)}$$

Let $\bar{\pi}$ be the profit level when $\alpha F_{K1} = r$, so that for $\alpha \geqslant r/F_{K1}$, $\pi \geqslant \bar{\pi}$. If absolute risk-aversion is non-increasing in profits, then $R_a'(\pi) \leqslant 0$, so that

$$R_a(\pi) \leqslant R_a(\bar{\pi}) \qquad \text{for } \alpha \geqslant r/F_{K1}.$$

Multiplying both sides by $(\alpha F_{K1} - r)$, we get

$$R_a(\pi)(\alpha F_{K1} - r) \leqslant R_a(\bar{\pi})(\alpha F_{K1} - r) \qquad \text{for } \alpha \geqslant r/F_{K1}. \qquad \text{(A.11)}$$

However, (A.11) holds for all α, because for $\alpha \leqslant r/F_{K1}$, $\pi < \bar{\pi}$, so that $R_a(\pi) \geqslant R_a(\bar{\pi})$. Then multiplying both sides with a non-positive expression $(\alpha F_{K1} - r)$ will yield (A.11). Thus

$$R_a(\pi)(\alpha F_{K1} - r) \leqslant R_a(\bar{\pi})(\alpha F_{K1} - r) \qquad \text{for all } \alpha. \qquad \text{(A.12)}$$

Substituting from (A.10) yields

$$U''(\alpha F_{K1} - r) \geqslant -R_a(\bar{\pi})U'(\alpha F_{K1} - r) \qquad \text{for all } \alpha. \qquad \text{(A.13)}$$

Applying the expectations operator to both sides of (A.13) and noting that $\bar{\pi}$, and hence $R_a(\bar{\pi})$, are given numbers, we obtain

$$E[U''(\alpha F_{K1} - r)] \geqslant -R_a(\bar{\pi})E[U'(\alpha F_{K1} - r)].$$

But from (2.4), $E[U'(\alpha F_{K1} - r)] = 0$. Hence

$$E[U''(\alpha F_{K1} - r)] \geqslant 0.$$

Q.E.D.

REFERENCES

[1] Batra, R. N., *Studies in the Pure Theory of International Trade* (London: Macmillan, 1973).
[2] ——, 'Resource Allocation in a General Equilibrium Model of Production Under Uncertainty', *Journal of Economic Theory*, 8 (May 1974) 50–63.
[3] Magee, S. P., 'Factor Market Distortions, Production, and Trade: A Survey', *Oxford Economic Papers*, 25 (Mar 1973) 1–42.
[4] Rybczynski, T. N., 'Factor Endowments and Relative Commodity Prices', *Economica*, 22 (Nov 1955) 336–41.

[5] Samuelson, P. A., 'International Factor Price Equalisation Once Again', *Economic Journal*, 59 (June 1949) 181–97.

[6] Stolper, W. F., and Samuelson, P. A., 'Protection and Real Wages', *Review of Economic Studies*, 9 (Nov 1941) 58–73. Reprinted in H. S. Ellis and L. A. Metzler (eds.), *Readings in the Theory of International Trade* (Philadelphia: Balkiston, 1949) 333–57.

3 The Heckscher–Ohlin Theory of International Trade Under Uncertainty

One of the most fundamental issues in international trade theory concerns the determination of a country's pattern of trade. The problem is to determine what goods a country will export or import. Stated differently, is it possible to prognosticate a country's configuration of importables or exportables just by examining the characteristics of its closed economy? The answer to this question defines not only a country's trade pattern but also the basis for the very presence of international trade. In other words, the explanation for the trade pattern is also, in general, an explanation for why a country trades at all.

The theory of the pattern of trade which has earned wide currency is popularly known as the Heckscher–Ohlin theorem. Associated with two Swedish economists, Eli Heckscher [4] and Bertil Ohlin [8], the theory asserts *that a country's exports use intensively its relatively abundant factor, and its imports use intensively its relatively scarce factor.* Thus, the Heckscher–Ohlin (H.O.) theory emphasises the role of a country's factor endowments in explaining the basis for its trade. Since its appearance in the early thirties, the H.O. theorem has received close scrutiny from several economists, but the implications of random elements for the validity of the theorem have not as yet been explored.

In this chapter, we specify the additional conditions needed to ensure the validity of the H.O. theorem in a stochastic environment. In the next chapter, our concern will be the investigation of the role played by these additional conditions in the derivation of the H.O. theorem.

3.1 Definitions of Factor Abundance

As suggested above, in explaining the basis for trade the H.O. theorem lays emphasis on the role played by differing factor endowments among countries. Evidently, the first step in the proof of the theorem is concerned with the way that we define international differences in factor endowments. Traditionally, the H.O. theorem has been derived in terms of two definitions of relative factor abundance, namely the 'factor-price' definition, which defines inter-country factor abundance in terms of the closed-economy factor-price ratios prevailing among countries, and the 'physical' definition, in which the supplies of primary factors to various countries are compared. Ideally, the H.O. theorem is supposed to apply to a multi-factor, multi-commodity, multi-country framework; but usually the theorem is derived from a two-country, two-factor, two-commodity model.

In this spirit, let us assume that there are only two countries, the home country (H) and the foreign country (F). If we further assume that there are only two primary factors, K and L, then according to the factor-price definition due initially to Heckscher and Ohlin, country H is capital-abundant (or labour-scarce) relative to country F if

$$\omega_h > \omega_f \tag{3.1}$$

where it may be reminded that ω denotes the wage/rental ratio, and the subscripts denote the countries. On the other hand, according to the physical definition due initially to Leontief [7], H is capital-abundant relative to F if

$$k_h > k_f \tag{3.2}$$

where $k = K/L$ is the overall capital/labour ratio. If the Heckscher–Ohlin dictum is true, then the capital-abundant home country should export the relatively capital-intensive commodity and import the relatively labour-intensive commodity from the labour-abundant foreign country.

Since the H.O. theorem dwells on the role played by international differences in factor endowments to explain the basis of international trade, it is natural for it to neglect various other possible reasons which could account for the existence of trade. For the full validity of the theorem, therefore, it is necessary to assume that in all other respects countries are alike. Thus, it is usually assumed that the home and foreign countries have identical technology and the structure of production, which in general includes (1) linearly homogeneous and concave production functions, (2) full employment of factors, (3) perfect competition in all internal markets, and finally, (4) non-reversible factor intensities, so that each commodity is intensive in the use of the same factor in both countries.

Our analysis in the next section first highlights the role played by these assumptions in the derivation of the H.O. theorem in terms of the factor-price definition and then goes on to show that this proof is untenable when uncertainty is introduced in one sector. Section 3.3 examines the theorem in terms of the physical definition, and there the results turn out to be more satisfactory.

3.2 The Factor-Price Definition and the H.O. Theorem

The proof of the H.O. theorem in terms of the factor-price definition requires the use of the unique relationship that exists between p and

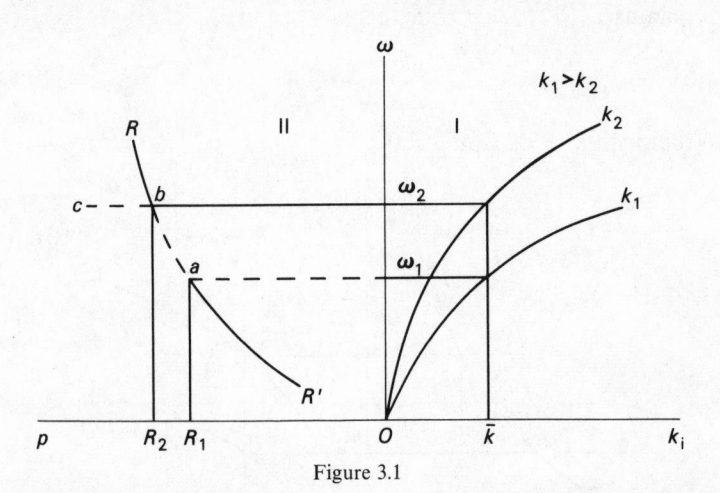

Figure 3.1

ω, a relationship that was first established by Samuelson [9] in terms of the deterministic two-sector model. In a way, this relationship has already been obtained in the previous chapter, where we showed that ω is affected only by p, provided that both goods are produced and X_1 firms are indifferent to risk. In so far as the certainty and the risk-neutrality cases yield identical results, Samuelson's one-to-one relationship between p and ω has then already been established in the foregoing chapter.

As stated above, the key to the derivation of the H.O. theorem from the factor-price definition is the existence of this unique relationship between p and ω. Consider Figs. 3.1 and 3.2, which depict this relation under two possibilities, depending on whether the first good is capital- or labour-intensive. The first quadrant of these diagrams displays the unique relationship between ω and the capital/labour ratio in each sector. The positive relation between ω and k_i in terms of the curves Ok_1 and Ok_2 reflects the reasoning that as the wage/rental ratio rises so that labour becomes relatively expensive, producers in all sectors respond by economising on the use of labour and by increasing the use of capital, and as a result, the capital/labour ratio rises in both industries. The same result can be derived by differentiating the equation furnishing

$$\omega = \frac{f_i - k_i f_i'}{f_i'} \tag{3.3}$$

to obtain†

$$\frac{dk_i}{d\omega} = -\frac{f_i'^2}{f_i f_i''} \tag{3.4}$$

so that with $f_i'' < 0$, $dk_i/d\omega > 0$.

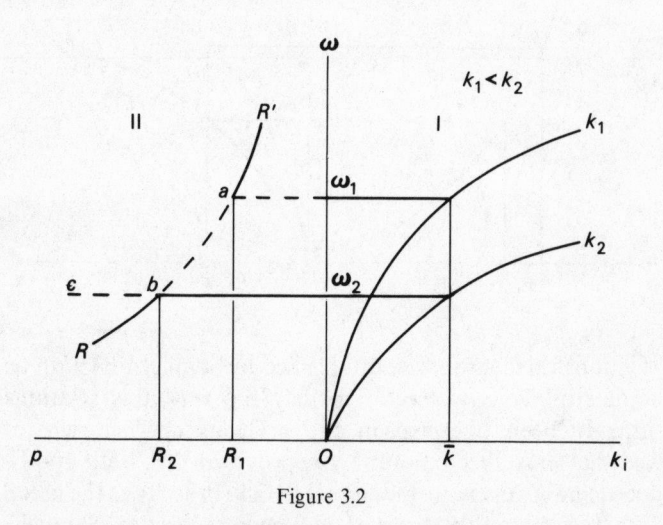

Figure 3.2

The location of the Ok_1 and Ok_2 curves in the diagrams determines the capital-intensity relationship between the two sectors, and through this, the slope of the RR' curve, which portrays the relationship between p and ω. In Fig. 3.1, $k_1 > k_2$ at all ω, so that RR' is

† As shown in the previous chapter, equation (3.3) is available in both the certainty and the uncertainty models.

positively inclined, indicating that as ω goes up, the relative price of the labour-intensive second good, p, also goes up, and conversely. By contrast, in Fig. 3.2 where $k_1 < k_2$ at all ω, RR' is negatively sloped to show that as ω goes up, the relative price of the capital-intensive second good, p, declines.

Not all points on the RR' curve are consistent with the constraint imposed by the full-employment condition. Suppose $O\overline{k}$ is the economy's overall capital/labour ratio. Then, the range of variation in ω – so long as both goods are to be produced in the economy – is given by $\omega_1\omega_2$. For, if at some ω, the capital/labour ratio in any industry comes to equal k, the output of the other industry falls to zero. This is amply clear from the fact that

$$k = \rho_1 k_1 + \rho_2 k_2 \qquad (3.5)$$

where $\rho_i = L_i/L$ and $\rho_1 + \rho_2 = 1$. Suppose that ω is given by $O\omega_1$ in the diagrams, then $k = k_1$, which from (3.5), implies that now $\rho_1 = 1$ and $\rho_2 = 0$, so that the output of the second good is also zero. Similarly, if ω is given by $O\omega_2$, $k = k_2$, in which case both factors will be fully employed in the second industry, and the output of the first industry will be zero. Any ω above $O\omega_2$ in Fig. 3.1, or above $O\omega_1$ in Fig. 3.2, is clearly not accessible to the economy, because it would require a k higher than $O\overline{k}$, whereas any ω below $O\omega_1$ in Fig. 3.1, or $O\omega_2$ in Fig. 3.2, conflicts with the full-employment constraint in that the weighted average of the capital/labour ratio in each sector will fall short of $O\overline{k}$. Hence, the range of variation in ω is determined by the economy's overall capital/labour ratio, as well as the Ok_1 and Ok_2 curves.

Corresponding to the variation-range of ω commensurate with the full-employment constraint is the variation-range of p. Evidently, if ω must vary between $O\omega_1$ and $O\omega_2$, p must vary between OR_1 and OR_2. Thus, the 'operational' range of the RR' curve is given by the dotted portion, $\omega_1 abc$. In other words, ω and p are no longer related after complete specialisation in any good is achieved.

It is now a simple matter to deduce the H.O. dictum from Figs. 3.1 and 3.2. In order to determine that there exists any basis for international trade, one needs to compare the autarky commodity-price ratios prevailing in the two countries. For, unless the autarky price ratios differ, trade will not occur. The countries would then produce goods at home rather than obtain them from abroad. What the H.O. theorem, in effect, says is that the autarky commodity-price

c

ratios differ in such a way that the country endowed relatively poorly with labour will find it more profitable to import the labour-intensive good and export the capital-intensive good. Therefore, given that the home country is capital-abundant relative to the foreign country, the H.O. theorem says that

$$p_h > p_f \quad \text{if } k_1 > k_2 \quad \text{and} \quad p_h < p_f \quad \text{if } k_2 > k_1. \quad (3.6)$$

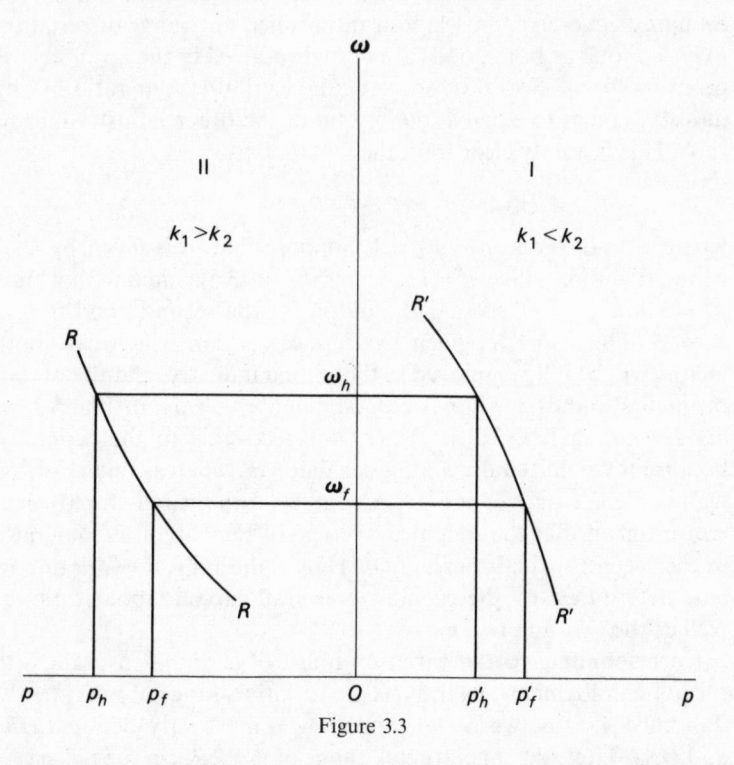

Figure 3.3

The proof of the H.O. theorem in terms of the factor-price definition then requires the derivation of the relations (3.6) from the definition given by (3.1). Consider Fig. 3.3, which reproduces parts of Figs. 3.1 and 3.2. The first quadrant of Fig. 3.3 portrays a negative relationship between p and ω in terms of the $R'R'$ curve under the condition that $k_2 > k_1$ at all ω, whereas the second quadrant depicts the positive relationship between p and ω in terms of the RR curve drawn for the case where $k_2 < k_1$ at all ω. Owing to the H.O. assumption of the international similarity of technology or production functions, RR or $R'R'$ curve describes the nature of the relationship between p and ω in both countries. $O\omega_h$ exceeds $O\omega_f$ to reflect the inter-country factor-endowment relationship expressed in (3.1), so that if

$$k_1 > k_2, \quad \text{then} \quad p_h > p_f$$

which implies that the home country will export the capital-intensive commodity X_1 and import the labour-intensive commodity X_2 from the foreign country, and if

$$k_1 < k_2, \quad \text{then} \quad p'_h < p'_f$$

and the home country will export X_2 and import X_1, but X_2 is now capital-intensive relative to X_1. Thus, whatever the factor-intensity relationship between the two commodities, the relatively capital-abundant country exports the relatively capital-intensive commodity and imports the relatively labour-intensive commodity from the relatively labour-abundant country.

This is how the H.O. theorem is customarily established in terms of the factor-price definition. The complications caused by the factor-intensity reversals are also usually considered, but since the reversibility of factor intensities is merely destructive of the full validity of the theorem, we will not pursue that subject here.

In addition to the absence of factor-intensity reversals, it is necessary to assume that there are no multiple international trade equilibria, because otherwise, as shown by Bhagwati [3], Inada [5], Kemp [6] and the author [1], the trade pattern may not follow the H.O. dictum even if the autarky price ratios differ in accordance with the theorem. However, this complication again is not germane to our discussion of uncertainty, which commences with the ensuing section.

3.3 The Factor-Price Definition and the H.O. Theorem Under Uncertainty

We will now show that the conventional proof of the H.O. theorem in terms of the factor-price definition is no longer acceptable in the presence of uncertainty in the economy. Ostensibly enough, the proof presented above relies on the fact that ω is related only to p and nothing else, so long as both goods are produced. If X_1 producers are apathetic towards risk, the suggested proof continues to be tenable, because in this case the characteristics of the deterministic, as well as the probabilistic models are essentially the same. However, if the producers are risk-averters, an assumption which comes closer to reality than does the risk-apathy assumption, then, as established in the preceding chapter, ω is related not only to p, but also to K and L. The direct consequence of this, as demonstrated below, is that the conventional proof of the H.O. theorem is no longer adequate.

In the foregoing chapter, we proved that (1) if K and L are constant, the relationship between ω and p is governed by the inter-industry factor-intensity relationship, provided that X_1 firms evince non-increasing absolute risk-aversion, and (2) if X_1 producers are risk-averters, then at constant p, w is positively related to K and negatively to L, whereas r is positively related to L and negatively to K. These results can be epitomised in the following equation:

$$\omega = \Psi(p, K, L) \tag{3.7}$$

with

$$\Psi_p \neq 0, \quad \Psi_K > 0 \quad \text{and} \quad \Psi_L < 0.$$

Let us now see whether in view of (3.7), the H.O. theorem can still be derived from the factor-price definition. First of all, the notion of international similarity of the production functions in our stochastic environment needs to be redefined. A simple definition suggests itself. *Suppose in both countries, $F_1(K_1, L_1)$ and $F_2(K_2, L_2)$ are the same, and α and its probability distribution are also the same, then production functions are identical internationally.* The reader may be critical of this definition because the assumption of the international similarity of the probability distribution of α is perhaps acceptable but, assuming that the actual values of α are the same in the two countries, is certainly far from innocuous. Unfortunately, there is no better alternative available.

A less restrictive definition of international identity of production functions would require that $F_i(K_i, L_i)$ and the probability distribution of α are the same in both countries; but then it is not legitimate to compare the actual autarky price ratios of the two countries and also expect the price-ratio comparisons to always be in line with the H.O. dictum. For, different actual values of α in the two countries could very easily compromise the validity of the H.O. theorem. Thus, so long as our concern is to evaluate the conventional, deterministic proofs of the H.O. theorem, it is necessary, and only reasonable, to assume that α is also the same in both countries.

There is one more aspect which must be examined before we proceed with our evaluation. The certainty proof of the H.O. theorem assumes, quite legitimately, that countries are alike in all other respects except the endowment of factor supplies. In the presence of uncertainty, this alikeness, in addition to similar technology and the production structure, must also include the international similarity of the utility functions from profits and the risk-attitudes of the X_1 producers. Accordingly, we also assume that producers in both countries have similar utility functions and are risk-averters.

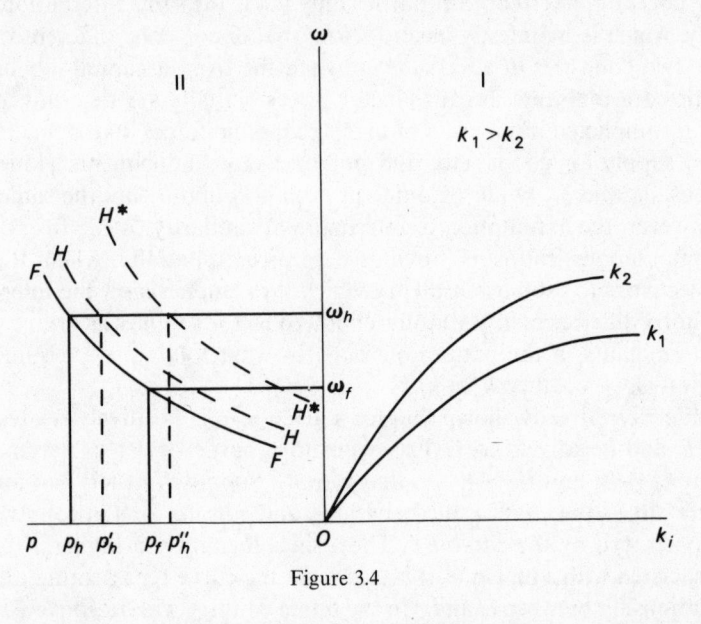

Figure 3.4

By now, we have laid the groundwork needed to appraise the customary derivation of the H.O. proposition in terms of the factor-price definition. Consider Fig. 3.4, where the first quadrant continues to depict the same positive relationship between ω and k_1 and k_2, because stochastic elements in the economy cause no alteration in equation (3.3) which equates the wage/rental ratio in the economy to the ratio of marginal products of the two factors in each sector. In the second quadrant, we depict, as before, the relationship between p and ω through the FF curve. If firms exhibit apathy towards risk, then the FF curve applies to both countries because of similar production functions, so that with $O\omega_h$ greater than $O\omega_f$

in conformity with the factor-price definition, $p_h > p_f$; the home country, in line with the H.O. hypothesis, will export the capital-intensive good X_1 and import the labour-intensive good X_2. This enables us to state the obvious: The H.O. theorem continues to hold in the presence of uncertainty, provided that firms are indifferent to risk.

If X_1 producers are risk-averse, then the FF curve does not represent the production structure in both countries, for ω is then related not only to p but also to k. Under risk-averse behaviour, the FF curve applies to both countries only if k is the same internationally, which is manifestly absurd. Note that ω could be different in the two countries in autarky even when the overall capital/labour ratios are the same, because factor prices actually are determined by a complicted interaction of many economic forces, like demand and supply for goods, etc., and not by factor endowments alone. Thus, ω_h and ω_f could be different even if k_h and k_f are the same. However, the assumption of international similarity of the overall capital/labour ratios is obviously bizarre, especially when the objective is to establish a theory which lays emphasis on the inter-country differences in 'naturally' endowed factor supplies as primary determinants of the pattern of trade. In what follows, we assume that if $\omega_h > \omega_f$, then $k_h > k_f$.†

We have already shown that for a given p, ω is positively related to K and negatively to L. For expository purposes, let us assume that $L_h = L_f$ and $K_h > K_f$, so that $k_h > k_f$. Suppose further, that for a certain k_f, the relationship between ω and p in the foreign country is portrayed by the curve FF. Then, since for any p, a higher K is associated with a higher ω, it is clear that the curve representing the relationship between ω and p in the home country will lie above FF towards the right. If k_h and k_f are not very different and the ω-p relationship in country H is depicted by curve HH, then the H.O. hypothesis continues to hold, since the home autarky price ratio, given by Op'_h, continues to exceed Op_f. However, if the difference between k_f and k_h is more pronounced and the ω–p relation in H is reflected by curve H^*H^*, then $p_h < p_f$ because $Op''_h < Op_f$, so that

---

† It is, of course, possible for k_h to be less than k_f when $\omega_h > \omega_f$, provided the autarky equilibria in the two countries are not unique. This, again, is a complication from which we must abstract, because our main concern is with the implications of uncertainty.

the capital-abundant home country, in contradiction of the H.O. dictum, will export the labour-intensive good X_2 and import the capital-intensive good X_1.

The story is little changed if $k_1 < k_2$, a case depicted in Fig. 3.5, where again the ω–p relation in H is expressed by curves HH or H^*H^*, depending on how different k_h is from k_f. Again, if the firms were risk-neutral, the home country would be exporting the capital-intensive good X_2 in exchange for the labour-intensive good X_1 from country F, because $p_h < p_f$. However, p_h may or may not be less than p_f, depending on whether the ω–p relation in H is furnished by curve HH or H^*H^*.

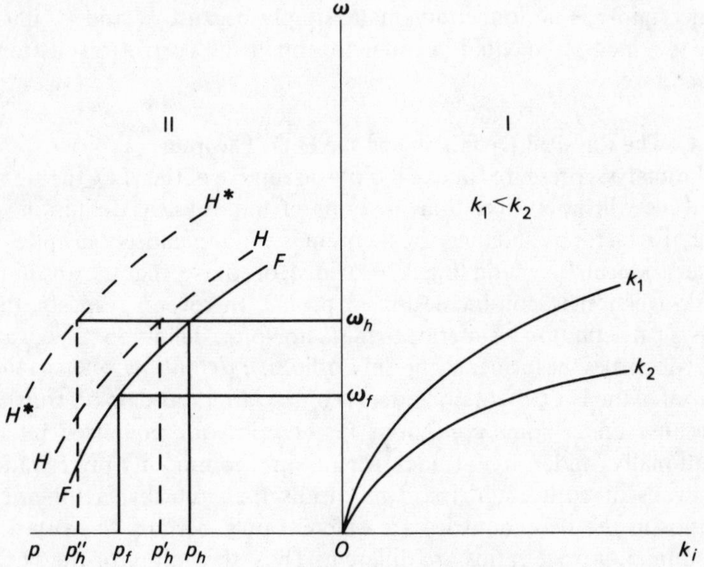

Figure 3.5

Can we then say that the H.O. theorem may not hold in the presence of the risk-averse behaviour? I am of the opinion that it is not legitimate to say that the H.O. theorem with risk-aversion is invalid, but that the proof of the theorem in terms of the factor-price definition is no longer adequate, and hence, is untenable. In the next section, we show that the H.O. theorem continues to hold without any modification provided relative factor abundance is defined in terms of the physical definition.

In the certainty case, ω is determined only by p, so that international differences in autarky price ratios are attributable only to differences in autarky levels of the ω's. The factor-price definition is also then the proper definition of relative factor abundance. However, in the presence of risk-averting behaviour by firms, ω is no longer independent of k, which implies that the factor-price definition is also no longer independent of k. Therefore, when the definition itself is dependent on some parameters, we should no longer expect the method of derivation of the theorem from that definition to furnish the correct analysis. Thus, our conclusion is that it is not proper to say that the H.O. theorem in terms of the factor-price definition may not hold, but that the customary proof in the presence of uncertainty is no longer adequate, simply because k_h and k_f must be assumed to be equal in order to obtain the correct result from the proof.

3.4   The Physical Definition and the H.O. Theorem

The analysis presented above is quite disruptive of the H.O. theorem, but we will now show that in terms of the physical definition of relative factor abundance, the theorem is valid in entirety in spite of the producers' aversion to risk, provided, of course, that the absolute risk-aversion is non-increasing in profits. In several respects, the physical definition is superior to the factor-price definition. Bhagwati [2] describes the former as the only 'objective' definition, whereas the proof of the H.O. theorem, in terms of the latter, borders on truism, because under some conditions factor prices are equalised internationally under free trade, where one commodity-price ratio prevails in both countries. This means that autarky factor-price ratios in the two countries are different only because the autarky commodity-price ratios are different. Thus, the failure of the H.O. theorem to hold under uncertainty in terms of the factor-price definition does not seem to be an irreparable loss, especially when, as it transpires, the theorem is fully valid in terms of the physical definition.

Customarily, in order to establish the H.O. theorem in terms of the physical definition, it is necessary, in addition to the assumptions already mentioned, to assume the international similarity of consumption patterns as well. Accordingly, we retain this assumption in our stochastic framework. Two countries are said to have the same consumption pattern, if at the same commodity-price ratio, they consume goods in the same proportion. In more technical terms, this means that the aggregate utility functions of the two countries are not only similar, but they are also homogeneous.

The verbal argument, which will presently be supplemented by a rigorous proof, behind the derivation of the H.O. theorem in terms of the physical definition can now be stated very succinctly. It is well known that there is an intimate link between the H.O. theorem and the Rybczynski effect, and since the latter, as established in the foregoing chapter, continues to hold in the presence of uncertainty and non-increasing absolute risk-aversion, the H.O. theorem also continues to hold without any modification. Consequential to the Rybczynski effect, the capital-abundant country produces relatively more of the capital-intensive commodity at any commodity-price ratio than does the labour-rich country, and if the consumption patterns are the same, then obviously the capital-abundant country will produce the capital-intensive commodity at a lower relative price than the other country, in which case the trade pattern will follow the H.O. dictum.

The initial argument presented above may now be supplemented by a rigorous geometrical proof. For expository convenience only, let us assume that the actual value of α, α^* equals $E[\alpha]$ in both countries. This enables us to use the concept of the expected transformation curve.†

Consider Fig. 3.6, which is drawn on the assumption that the first good is capital-intensive relative to the second; HH' is the home transformation curve, which, because the home country is more endowed than the foreign country with physical amounts of capital relative to labour, is shown to be biased towards the actual (equal to the expected, when $\alpha^* = \mu$) output of the first good, whereas FF', the foreign country's transformation curve, is biased towards the labour-intensive good X_2. Two community indifference curves, one for each country, are introduced to determine the closed-economy or the self-sufficiency equilibrium, which for H, lies at S_h and for F, at S_f.‡ The assumption of international similarity of the consumption pattern enters into the analysis through the fact that the two indifference curves are non-intersecting. The relative price of the

---

† It is worth pointing out here that the derivation of the H.O. theorem does not depend on this assumption.

‡ How the closed-economy equilibrium is determined under risk-averse behaviour has been discussed in detail in Chapter 2.

second good is given by the slope of AB at S_h and of CD at S_f. Since AB is steeper than CD, it is clear that

$$p_h > p_f$$

so that the capital-abundant home country will export the capital-intensive good X_1 and import the labour-intensive good X_2. This proves the H.O. proposition.

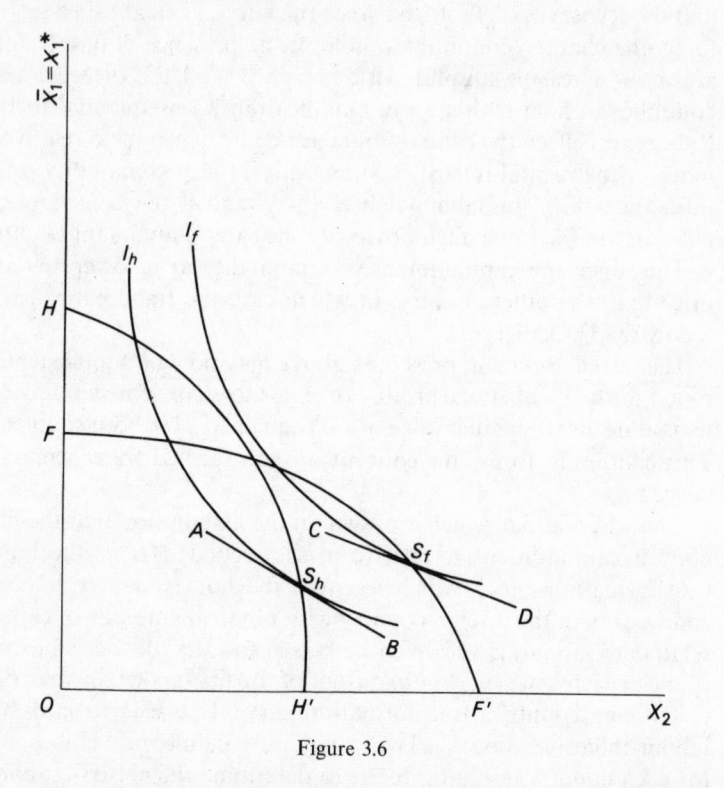

Figure 3.6

A similar proof is available for the case where $k_1 < k_2$. It is worth noting that the assumption of $\alpha^* = \mu$ is not crucial to the derivation of the H.O. theorem in terms of the physical definition.

Until now, we have assumed that although α is a random variable, its realised value is the same in the two countries. This is admittedly a very restrictive assumption, but without it, the international identity of production functions cannot be assured. On the other hand, if one is willing to make the weaker assumption that μ (not α)

is the same in both countries, then evidently only the expected and not the actual pattern of trade can be predicted along the lines suggested by the H.O. hypothesis. The theorem may then be restated as follows: *A country is expected to export a commodity which is intensive in the use of its abundant factor.*

3.5 Summary

The objective of this chapter has been to analyse the validity—in the presence of uncertainty—of the Heckscher–Ohlin theorem, which states that a country's exports are intensive in the use of its relatively abundant factor. In pursuit of this goal, we have drawn heavily on the results established in the preceding chapter. Our principal results are as follows:

1. The customary proof of the H.O. theorem in terms of the factor-price definition – which defines inter-country factor abundance by comparing the autarky factor-price ratios in the two countries – is not tenable in the presence of risk-averse behaviour by producers, because in the latter case, factor prices are determined not only by commodity prices but also by factor supplies.

2. In terms of the physical definition of relative factor abundance – which makes comparisons between the physical supplies of primary factors to each country – the H.O. theorem continues to hold with undiminished glory, provided we assume that absolute risk-aversion is non-increasing in profits, an assumption which is usually considered to be realistic.

REFERENCES

[1] Batra, R. N., *Studies in the Pure Theory of International Trade* (London: Macmillan, 1973) chap. 3.

[2] Bhagwati, J. N., 'Protection, Real Wages and Real Incomes', *Economic Journal*, 69 (Dec 1959) 735–48.

[3] ——, 'The Proofs of the Theorems on Comparative Advantage', *Economic Journal*, 77 (Mar 1967) 75–83.

[4] Heckscher, E. F., 'The Effect of Foreign Trade on the Distribution of Income', in H. S. Ellis and L. A. Metzler (eds.), *Readings in the Theory of International Trade* (Philadelphia: Balkiston, 1949).

[5] Inada, K., 'A Note on the Heckscher-Ohlin Theorem', *Economic Record*, 106 (Mar 1967) 88–96.

[6] Kemp, M. C., *The Pure Theory of International Trade and Investment* (New Jersey: Prentice-Hall, 1969) chap. 3.

[7] Leontief, W. W., 'Domestic Production and Foreign Trade: The American Capital Position Re-examined', *Economia Internazionale*, 7 (Feb 1954) 3–32.
[8] Ohlin, B., *Interregional and International Trade* (Cambride, Mass.: Harvard University Press, 1933).
[9] Samuelson, P. A., 'International Factor-Price Equalization Once Again', *Economic Journal*, 59 (June 1949) 181–97.

4 Uncertainty and the Properties of the Heckscher–Ohlin Model

While establishing the validity of the Heckscher–Ohlin (H.O.) proposition in the presence of risk-averse behaviour by producers, we introduced a number of assumptions in addition to those which are usually maintained for this type of analysis. It is high time that we justify these assumptions, which required α, its probability distribution, and the producers' attitudes towards risk to be the same in both countries. Our defence, of course, is the fact that without these assumptions the H.O. theorem may not hold in our stochastic model.

It should be mentioned at the outset that, however unrealistic it may be to assume the international equality of α, it is not possible to do without this specification because otherwise the basic assumption of the H.O. hypothesis, namely, the international identity of production functions, will be violated. However, although in the interest of international similarity of production functions, the actual level of α must be assumed to be the same in both countries, the same vindication cannot apply to the assumption regarding the inter-country similarity of the probability distribution of α, and since the latter is a subjective concept, one that reflects the subjective beliefs of the producers about the random variable, it could very easily differ from one country to the other. Similarly, the risk-attitudes of producers could be markedly different among the countries.

The next three sections of this chapter are devoted to the investigation of the implications for the H.O. theorem of the international dissimilarity of (1) the distribution of α, and (2) the producers' disposition to risk. In the latter sections, we explore the consequences of uncertainty for the factor-price equalisation theorem which is an intrinsic property of the deterministic H.O. model.

4.1 Resource Allocation and the Probability Distribution of α

We have already indicated above that the distribution of α could very easily vary from one country to the other. For instance, suppose the first sector is the agricultural sector and α represents the random influence of rainfall. Depending on the weather and the climatic conditions, the distribution of α is likely to differ among the countries because the farmers' expectations about the level and spread of the rainfall are most probably different from country to country.

At another level of generality, suppose α represents not the rainfall but the annual quantity of water available for irrigation through rains, rivers, canals, tube-wells, etc. Note that α is still a random variable, but its randomness can be reduced by increased use of man-made irrigation facilities offered free by the government.† In developed countries like the United States, Canada, Australia, etc., the expected value of α is likely to be higher and its variance lower than their corresponding levels in some underdeveloped countries like India, Pakistan, Sri Lanka, etc., where there is heavy dependence on rains.

The case of agriculture apart, suppose that α represents the influence of industrial strikes which differ in frequency and duration from country to country. Here again then, the expected value, as well as the variance of α, may vary from one country to the other. In Britain, for example, where trade unions are powerful, α is likely to have a lower expected value (representing longer duration of strikes) and a higher variance (representing a greater frequency of strikes or a greater number of wildcat strikes); whereas in Germany, where trade unions are more disciplined or perhaps subdued, α is likely to have a higher mean and a lower variance.

The question arises: Do such differences have any influence on the validity of the H.O. theorem even when internationally α is the same? The answer is an unqualified Yes, because the mean and the variance of α affect the decision-making of X_1 producers who encounter uncertainty. At the time of decision-making, α is unknown to producers, so that their input–output decisions are guided by their subjective probability distribution of α. This eventually affects the allocation of resources in the entire economy.

In order to develop this line of reasoning further, we first need to investigate the effects of a change in the distribution of α at

† The free supply of irrigation facilities is assumed just for the sake of argument. It may or may not in effect be true, but this assumption eliminates the need to consider the possibility of investment in irrigation facilities by the individual producer, which will mitigate the effect of uncertainty about the availability of water.

constant p and k on the output of X_2 and the expected, or even the actual, output of X_1. As a rule, anything that influences the expected output of X_1 will also affect its actual or realised output.

With this purpose in mind, we rewrite the seven basic equations which specified our stochastic model in Chapter 2. These equations, which include equations (2.1), (2.5), (2.8)–(2.11) and (2.12), are

$$X_1 = \alpha L_1 f_1(k_1) \tag{4.1}$$

$$X_2 = L_2 f_2(k_2) \tag{4.2}$$

$$(f_1 - k_1 f_1')E[U'\alpha] = p(f_2 - k_2 f_2')E[U'] \tag{4.3}$$

$$f_1'E[U'\alpha] = pf_2'E[U'] \tag{4.4}$$

$$L_1 + L_2 = L \tag{4.5}$$

$$L_1 k_1 + L_2 k_2 = K \tag{4.6}$$

and

$$\pi = L_1[\alpha_1 f_1 - p(f_2 - k_2 f_2') - pk_1 f_2']. \tag{4.7}$$

In order to discover the effects of a change in the distribution of α, let us write $\hat{\alpha}$ as

$$\hat{\alpha} = \gamma\alpha + \theta$$

where γ and θ are the shift parameters initially equal to one and zero respectively. As explained in Chapter 1, an increase in the mean alone is represented by an increase in θ, whereas an increase in the variance alone is displayed by an upward shift in γ, along with a downward shift in θ such that $d\theta/d\gamma = -\mu$.

Let us now see how a shift in γ and θ affect X_2 and the expected output of X_1, when p, K and L are kept constant. Replacing α by $\hat{\alpha}$ and differentiating (4.3)–(4.7) with respect to γ, and remembering that initially $p = 1$, $\gamma = 1$ and $\theta = 0$, we obtain the following system of equations:

$$\begin{pmatrix} A_1 & B_1 & C_1 \\ A_2 & B_2 & C_2 \\ (k_1 - k_2) & L_1 & L_2 \end{pmatrix} \begin{pmatrix} dL_1 \\ dk_1 \\ dk_2 \end{pmatrix} = \begin{pmatrix} Q_1 \\ Q_2 \\ 0 \end{pmatrix} \tag{4.8}$$

where A_i, B_i and C_i ($i = 1, 2$) denote the same expressions as in (2.15) in Chapter 2, and where

$$Q_1/\omega = Q_2 = -f_2'E[L_1(k_1+\omega)U''h_1 + U'(\alpha d\gamma + d\theta)] \quad (4.9)$$

and

$$h_1 = (\alpha F_{K1} - r).$$

It may be noted that the derivation of the system (4.8) proceeds exactly along the lines followed in the text and appendix of Chapter 2, except that now K, L and p are fixed, and γ and θ are allowed to vary. The solution of equation (4.8), in view of (2.15), yields:

$$dk_1 = \frac{(\omega C_2 - C_1)(k_1 - k_2)Q_2}{D} \quad (4.10)$$

$$dk_2 = \frac{(B_1 - \omega B_2)(k_1 - k_2)Q_2}{D} \quad (4.11)$$

and

$$dL_1 = -\frac{[L_2(B_1 - \omega B_2) + L_1(\omega C_2 - C_1)]Q_2}{D} \quad (4.12)$$

where D is the denominator of the system (4.8), and as demonstrated in the appendix to Chapter 2, $D > 0$ under non-increasing absolute risk-aversion. Similarly, in Chapter 2, we established in (2.20) and (2.21) that

$$\omega C_2 - C_1 = C = -f_2''(k_2 + \omega)E[U'] \quad (4.13)$$

and

$$B_1 - \omega B_2 = B = -f_1''(k_1 + \omega)E[U'\alpha] \quad (4.14)$$

are both positive.

It is now a relatively simple matter to examine the influence of γ and θ on the two outputs. The expected output of the first good from (4.1) is given by

$$\bar{X}_1 = (\mu\gamma + \theta)L_1 f_1(k_1). \quad (4.15)$$

Differentiating this totally, we obtain

$$d\bar{X}_1 = (\mu d\gamma + d\theta)L_1 f_1 + \mu[L_1 f_1' dk_1 + f_1 dL_1]$$

again remembering that initially $\gamma = 1$ and $\theta = 0$.

Substituting for dk_1 and dL_1 from (4.10) and (4.12) in this expression, and using (4.13) and (4.14), we get

$$d\overline{X}_1 = (\mu d\gamma + d\theta)L_1 f_1 - \frac{\mu}{D}[L_1 C(\omega + k_2)f_1' + L_2 f_1 B]Q_2. \quad (4.16)$$

Similarly, we get

$$dX_2 = \frac{[L_2 B(\omega + k_1)f_2' + L_1 f_2 C]Q_2}{D}. \quad (4.17)$$

Let us first examine the effects of an increase in θ alone. Here $d\theta > 0$, whereas $d\gamma = 0$. With this, the sign of all the terms in (4.16) and (4.17), except Q_2, is determined. The sign of Q_2 in turn is determined among other things, by the sign of $E[U''h_1]$ which in Chapter 2 was demonstrated to be non-negative under the hypothesis of non-increasing absolute risk-aversion. Thus, with this latter proviso and with $d\theta > 0$ and $d\gamma = 0$, Q_2 from (4.9) is clearly negative, which means that $d\overline{X}_1 > 0$ and $dX_2 < 0$. The same result obviously holds when the firms are indifferent to risk.

The economic explanation of this result is as follows. It was demonstrated in Chapter 1 that risk-averse firms hire inputs in such a way that the value of the expected marginal product of each factor remains above the input price. An increase in the expected value of α then raises the expected marginal product of both factors in the same proportion and thus acts like a Hicks-neutral technical advance,† which – in the deterministic model – is well known to culminate, at constant p, K and L, in a rise in the output of the good enjoying the technical change, and a decline in the output of the other good.‡ A similar effect is taking place in our stochastic model, although a rise in the expected value of α is by no means the same thing as technical progress. However, for $\overline{X}_1$ to rise unambiguously, we also need non-increasing absolute risk-aversion, because an increase in the mean of α contributes to more sanguine expectations of profits on the part of producers, so that as the risk-aversion declines, X_1 producers also lower the spread between the factor prices and the value of the expected marginal products of both factors, which in turn leads to a further rise in $\overline{X}_1$. The increase in $\overline{X}_1$ in turn pulls resources away from X_2 and hence causes a decline in the output of X_2.

Figure 4.1 illustrates this result diagrammatically. The original

† It is well known that a Hicks-neutral technical improvement is defined by an equiproportionate increase in the marginal productivity of both factors. See Hicks [2].

‡ See, for example, Batra [1, chap. 6].

expected transformation curve is given by TT', but as $E[\alpha]$ increases, TT' shifts to GT' – reflecting an increase in the maximum possible level of $\overline{X}_1$ from OT to OG, with no increase in the maximal output level of X_2. The production point prior to the rise in μ is P, whereas that after the rise is P', where AB is parallel to CD to show that the commodity-price ratio is constant. The comparison of output levels associated with P with those prevailing at P' confirms the result derived just above. The difference between Figs. 4.1a and b is that the former depicts the case of risk-indifference, whereas the latter portrays the case of non-increasing absolute risk-aversion. Finally, it is easy to see that in the case of a decline in μ, the results are merely reversed.

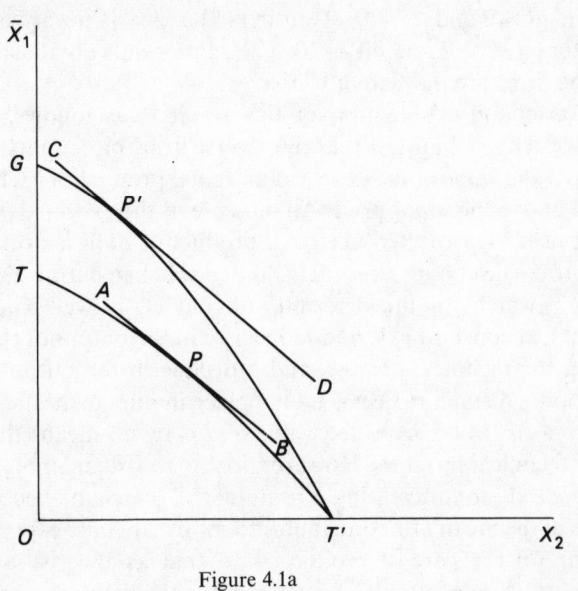

Figure 4.1a

Next, we examine the implication for the two outputs of an increase in the variance of α while its mean is kept constant, which, as stated earlier, requires that $d\theta/d\gamma = -\mu$. Making this substitution in (4.16) and (4.9) then yields

$$d\overline{X}_1 = -\frac{\mu[L_1 C(\omega + k_2)f_1' + L_2 f_1 B]Q_2}{D} \tag{4.18}$$

and

$$Q_2 = -f_2' E[\{L_1(k_1 + \omega)U''h_1 + U'\}(\alpha - \mu)]d\gamma. \tag{4.19}$$

As regards dX_2, the only thing that changes in (4.17) is the expression for Q_2, which is, of course, given by (4.19).

Once again, the sign of Q_2 plays an important role in determining the sign of $d\overline{X}_1$ and dX_2. This, however, is not clear any more, and we have to perform some manipulations on (4.19).

Let us separate the two components of (4.19) as

$$Q_2 = -f_2'E[U''h_1(\alpha-\mu)]L_1(k_1+\omega)d\gamma$$
$$- f_2'E[U'(\alpha-\mu)]d\gamma. \tag{4.19*}$$

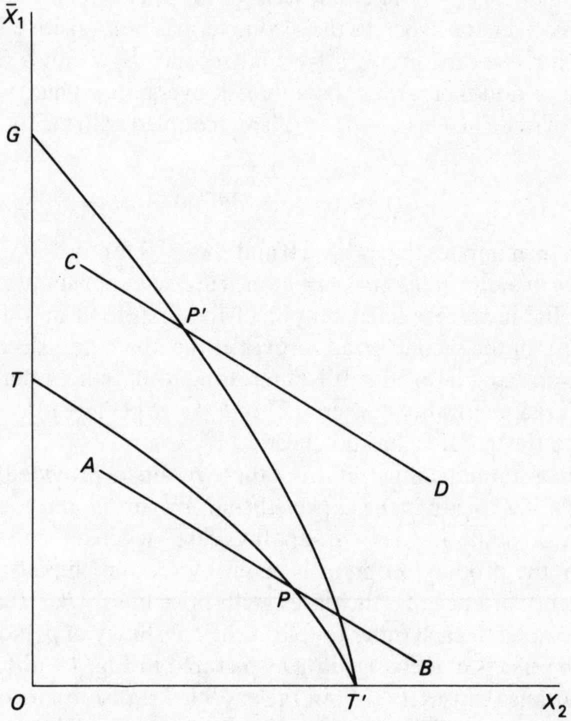

Figure 4.1b

The sign of $E[U'(\alpha-\mu)]$ is non-positive because

$$E[U'(\alpha-\mu)] = E[U']E[\alpha-\mu]+\text{cov}[U',(\alpha-\mu)]$$
$$= \text{cov}[U',(\alpha-\mu)] \tag{4.20}$$

and the covariance between U' and $(\alpha - \mu)$ is negative in view of the fact that $U''(\pi) < 0$ under risk-aversion and $\partial \pi / \partial \alpha > 0$. The sign of $E[U'' h_1 (\alpha - \mu)]$ can also be shown to be negative under non-increasing absolute risk-aversion, but some care has to be exercised in the proof. We can write

$$
\begin{aligned}
E[U'' h_1 (\alpha - \mu)] &= E\left[U'' h_1 \left(\alpha - \frac{r}{F_{K1}} + \frac{r}{F_{K1}} - \mu \right) \right] \\
&= E\left[\frac{U'' h_1^2}{F_{K1}} \right] + \frac{(r - \mu F_{K1})}{F_{K1}} E[U'' h_1] \qquad (4.21)
\end{aligned}
$$

because $h_1 = \alpha F_{K1} - r$. The first term of (4.21) is evidently negative under risk-aversion, whereas the second term is non-positive because first, with risk-aversion $r \leqslant \mu F_{K1}$, and second, $E[U'' h_1] \geqslant 0$ in the presence of non-increasing absolute risk-aversion.† Thus, with the latter proviso, $E[U'' h_1 (\alpha - \mu)] < 0$. This, coupled with (4.20), implies that

$$
Q_2 > 0 \quad \text{for} \quad d\gamma > 0
$$

which in turn implies that $d\overline{X}_1 < 0$ and $dX_2 > 0$ for $d\gamma > 0$. In other words, *an increase in the variance* alone causes, at constant p, K and L, a decline in the expected output of the first good and a rise in the output of the second good, provided the absolute risk-aversion is non-increasing in profits. It is interesting to note here that in the case of risk-neutrality, where $E[U'' h_1] = E[U'(\alpha - \mu)] = 0$, the change in the variance has no effect on $\overline{X}_1$ and X_2.

The diagrammatic illustration of these results is provided by Fig. 4.2, where TT' again is the expected transformation curve, P is the production point in the risk-apathy case, whereas under risk-aversion, the production point is given by P', and the latter shifts to P'' as the variance of α increases, with price lines AB, CD and EF drawn parallel to each other to reflect the constancy of p. Note that, unlike the effects of a change in μ as pictured in Fig. 4.1, the change in the variance causes no shift in the expected transformation curve.

Before we proceed any further, a brief recapitulation of the results obtained in this section is in order. The analysis presented above shows that an increase in the expected value of α causes an increase

---

† Remember that risk-averse producers hire inputs in such a way that the value of the expected marginal productivity of each factor exceeds the input price. For further details, see Chapter 1.

in $\bar{X}_1$ and a decline in X_2, and vice versa, provided (1) the firms are risk-neutral, or (2) they have non-increasing absolute risk-aversion. In contrast, an increase in the variance of α stimulates a rise in X_2 and a decline in $\bar{X}_1$, and conversely, provided again that firms have non-increasing absolute risk-aversion. This last result is not available in the risk-apathy case.

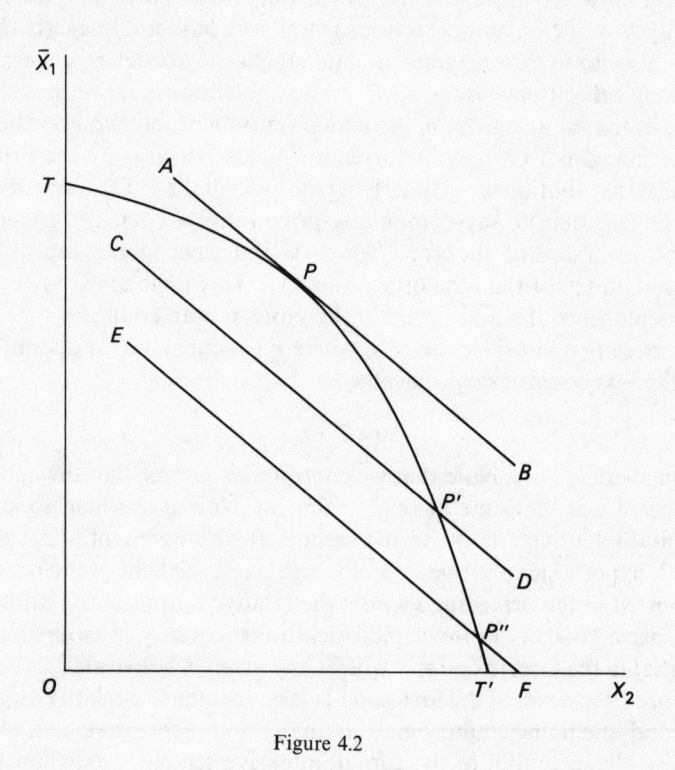

Figure 4.2

Until now, our concern in this section has been with the expected output of the first good. Needless to say, the results derived above are applicable, without any qualification, to the actual or realised output of the first good. This is because the actual value of α plays no role in the decision-making by X_1 producers, whereas the results derived so far in this chapter, and others, depend solely on the input–output decisions of the firms constituting both industries.

4.2   Distribution of α and the H.O. Theorem

With our prognosis in the preceding section, we are analytically equipped to investigate the implications of the international dissimilarity of the probability distribution of α for the validity of the H.O. hypothesis. The general result, which may have become palpable by now, is that the H.O. theorem may no longer hold.

The intuitive argument for this deduction is fairly simple. The analysis of the foregoing section, as well as Chapter 2, suggests that the allocation of resources in our stochastic model is governed among other things by p, K, L, μ and the variance (v) of α, which means that at any given p, the actual outputs of the two goods are determined not only by factor endowments but also by the probability distribution of α. Underlying the logic of the H.O. proposition is the fact that at any commodity-price ratio, a country produces relatively more of the good which is intensive in the use of its abundant factor than the other country.† This logic may, however, be demolished if μ and v are not the same in both countries.

Let us first consider the case where v is similar but μ dissimilar in the two countries. Specifically, let

$$\mu_h > \mu_f \tag{4.22}$$

along with $v_h = v_f$. Note that we continue to assume that the actual value of α is the same in both countries. Now if the first good is capital-intensive relative to the second, then, in view of (4.22), the H.O. hypothesis continues to hold, because in the light of the results reported in the preceding section, the relative output of the capital-intensive good X_1 in the capital-rich home country in comparison to that in the foreign country will, at any given p, be even larger than before.‡ However, if the first good is labour-intensive relative to the second, the home country may, at any p, no longer produce a relatively higher output of the capital-intensive second good than the foreign country, in which case the theorem may or may not hold.

A geometrical illustration of the counter example to the H.O. theorem is furnished by Fig. 4.3 where HH' and FF' are respectively the home and the foreign transformation curves representing loci of realised outputs of X_1 and X_2 and the case where $\mu_h = \mu_f$ and

---

† See the arguments presented in section 3.4 in the preceding chapter.
‡ Remember that we are now talking about the actual or realised outputs.

$k_2 > k_1$.† For the sake of simplicity of construction, initially only one community indifference curve, I_1, is introduced to represent the demand conditions in both countries, so that the autarky equilibrium point in country F is S_f and that in country H is S_h, with the autarky

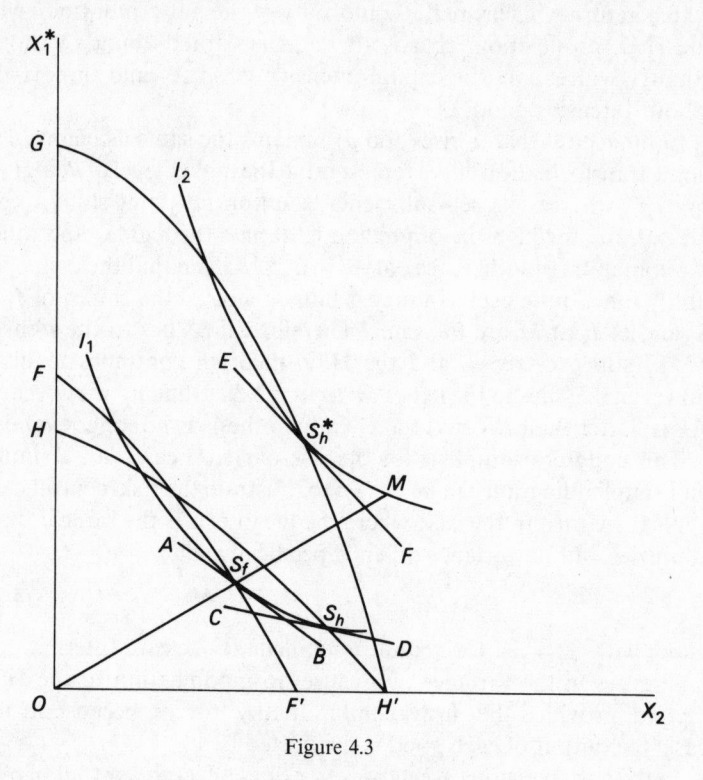

Figure 4.3

† In Chapter 2, the properties of the actual and the expected transformation curve were found to be similar except that, from (2.39),

$$\frac{dX_1^*}{dX_2} = -\frac{\alpha^* E[U']}{\mu E[U'] + \text{cov}(U', \alpha)} = -\beta^* p$$

where the asterisk, as before, denotes the actual or realised values. With $\alpha^* \neq \mu$, it is not clear what the value of β^* is. However, in the construction of Fig. 4.3 and 4.4, we assume that $\beta^* > 1$, although the current arguments are not sensitive to this assumption.

The reader may also be reminded here that since the home country is capital-abundant relative to the foreign country, $k_2 > k_1$, and α^* is the same in both countries, the actual transformation curve of the home country, HH', is biased towards X_2, and that of the foreign country is biased towards X_1^*. This, of course, is necessarily true only in the initial situation where the probability distribution of α is the same in both countries.

relative price of the second good in the two countries displayed by the slopes of AB and CD. Since AB is steeper than CD,

$$p_f > p_h$$

which in turn will ensure the conformity of the pattern of trade with the H.O. proposition; that is to say, the capital-abundant home country will export the capital-intensive good X_2 and import the labour-intensive good X_1.

Assume now, that μ_h rises and μ_f remains the same as before. The home transformation curve representing the higher level of μ_h is given by GH', whereas its self-sufficiency equilibrium point shifts to S_h^*. Draw a ray through the origin and let it pass through S_f and touch the community indifference curve, I_2, at M. Given that the aggregate utility function in each country is homogeneous, the slopes of I_1 at S_f and of I_2 at M are the same. Therefore, if S_h^* lies to the right of M, p_f still exceeds p_h, and the H.O. theorem continues to hold; however, if S_h^* lies to the left of M, as in the diagram, $p_f < p_h$ because AB is flatter than EF, and the H.O. hypothesis is no longer valid.

This counter-example is for the risk-aversion case, but a similar and simpler diagram can be drawn to illustrate the risk-neutral case.

Next we turn to the case where the mean of α is the same in both countries, but its variance differs. Specifically, let

$$v_h < v_f \tag{4.23}$$

along with $\mu_h = \mu_f$. One result is immediately clear: International differences in the variance of α cause no modification to the H.O. dictum, provided that firms exhibit apathy to risk, because in this case, the output of each good is unaffected by v.

In the risk-aversion case, however, v does affect the output of each good, which in turn puts the validity of the H.O. hypothesis in jeopardy. As established in the previous section, the economy allocates a higher proportion of its resources to the first industry as the variance of α declines. This means that the capital-abundant home country at any p will continue to produce a relatively larger output of X_1 than will the foreign country, provided $k_1 > k_2$. In the contrary case of $k_1 < k_2$, however, this result is no longer certain, and, as a consequence, the H.O. theorem may not hold.

Figure 4.4 provides a diagrammatical demonstration of this conclusion. As in Fig. 4.3, S_h and S_f are the autarky equilibrium points in the two countries in the case where $v_h = v_f$ and $\mu_h = \mu_f$, so that

$p_f > p_h$. A lower variance of α in the home country at the original mean, however, shifts the home production, and hence the self-sufficiency equilibrium point, along HH' to the left of S_h. Thus, in Fig. 4.4, S_h^* is the equilibrium point associated with the lower v_h, and since S_h^* lies to the left of M, $p_f < p_h$, and the H.O. theorem no longer holds.

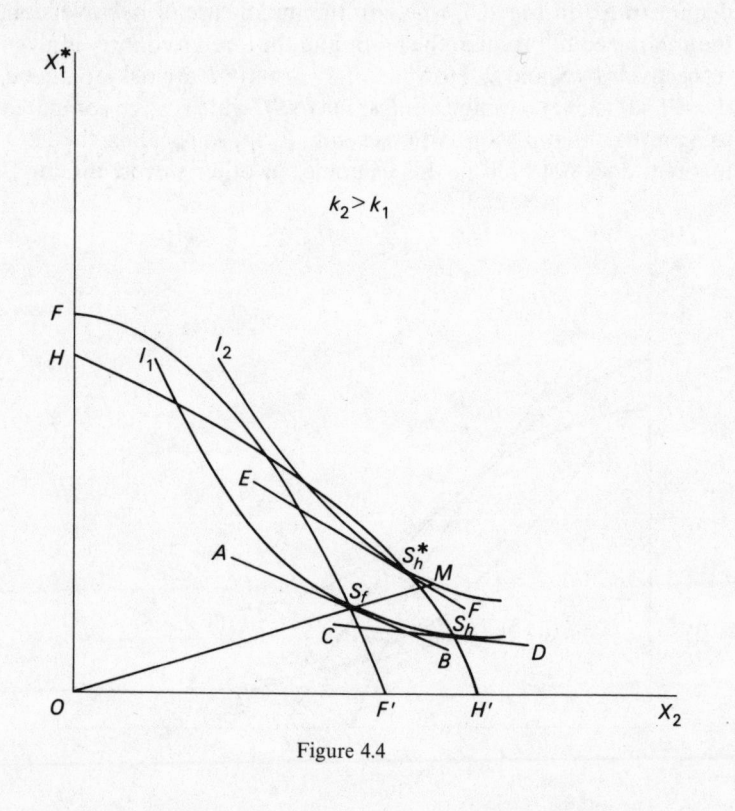

Figure 4.4

4.3 Risk-Attitudes of the Producers and the H.O. Theorem

Our analysis in the preceding section shows that international differences in the probability distribution of α endanger the validity of the H.O. theorem, even if the model satisfies all other assumptions including that requiring the similarity of producers' utility functions in the two countries.

In the present section, we relax the latter assumption and show how the H.O. logic may be demolished in spite of the fulfilment of all other assumptions. Specifically, we assume that X_1 producers in the foreign country are risk-neutral, but those in the home country are risk-averse. In addition, we assume that $\alpha^* = \mu$ in each country. In the foreign country then, resource allocation is not influenced by uncertainty, whereas in the home country, it is. If $k_2 > k_1$, the H.O. theorem will still be valid; however, if $k_1 > k_2$, it may not, as demonstrated in Fig. 4.5, where in the initial case of risk-aversion, the autarky equilibrium in the home and the foreign country is given respectively by S_h and S_f. However, if X_1 firms in F are risk-apathetic, the self-sufficiency equilibrium F shifts to S_f^*, which, when compared to S_h, reveals that $p_f > p_h$, whereas initially, $p_f < p_h$. Thus, the H.O. theorem does not hold in this example. In other words, the inter-

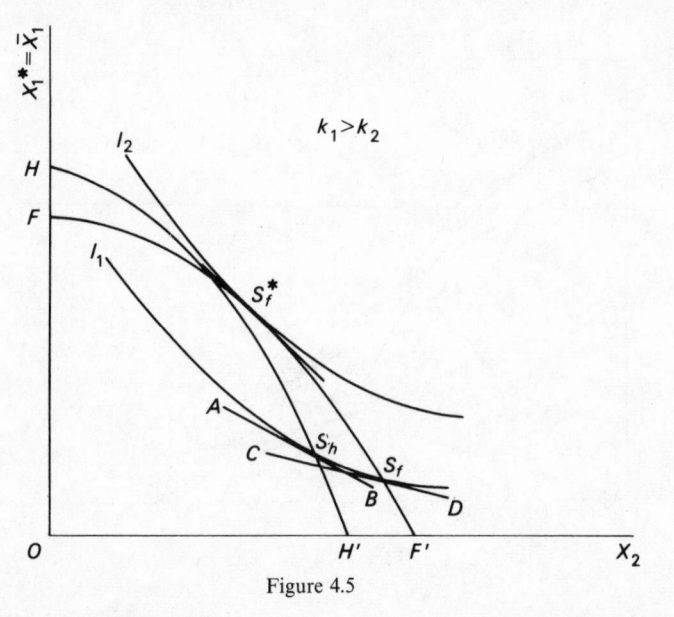

Figure 4.5

national similarity of producers' utility functions from profits is one of the conditions sufficient to ensure the validity of the H.O. theorem in the presence of uncertainty.

4.4 Uncertainty and the Likelihood of Complete Specialisation
It has been argued by several trade theorists that if the physical factor endowments of the two countries are very different, the exposure of the economies to international trade may stimulate

each country to specialise completely in production of its exportable good.† We will now show that in the presence of risk-averse behaviour, uncertainty contributes to a decline in the likelihood of complete specialisation in exportables.

A simple demonstration of this point requires first an examination of the customary logic which is illustrated in Fig. 4.6. This diagram is a replica of Fig. 3.3; as before, quadrant I of Fig. 4.6 depicts the positive relationship between ω and k_i under the stipulation of $k_1 > k_2$; the second quadrant, on the other hand, pictures the positive relationship between p and ω.

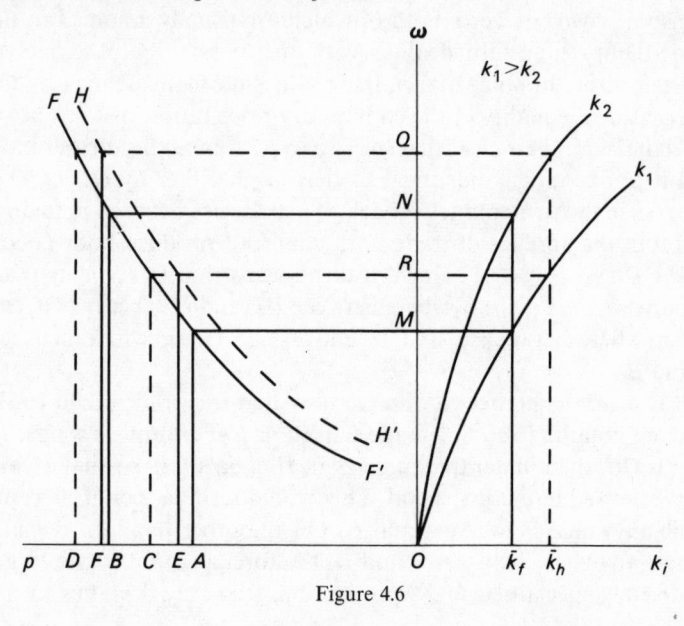

Figure 4.6

Consider first the case of certainty or of risk-neutrality on the part of producers. Here only one curve, namely FF', depicts the ω–p relation in both countries. The overall capital/labour ratio in country F is given by $O\bar{k}_f$, and that in H by $O\bar{k}_h$. The overall k in each country determines, in conjunction with the Ok_1 and Ok_2 curves, the variation-range of each country's ω (such as MN and RQ) under the condition that both goods are produced. Corresponding to the variation-range of ω in each country is the variation-range of p,

† See Johnson [3, chap. 1], among many others.

which is commensurate with incomplete specialisation. Thus, the variation-range of p in the foreign country is given by AB, and that in the home country by CD.

Note that a comprehension of how the variation-range of p is determined is important in understanding whether or not the introduction of international trade may lead the trading country to complete specialisation in exportables. As the two countries are exposed to international trade, there comes to prevail only one commodity-price ratio in both countries, provided there are no interventions in the free flow of goods across the countries and the transport costs are zero, both of which are usually assumed in the trade-theory literature dealing with the possibility of complete specialisation. In point of fact, free trade is normally defined by the international equality of the commodity-price ratios.

At the outset, it is clear that the free trade commodity-price ratio – call it p^* – cannot be identical to that given either by OD or OA, because in the two-country model, p^* usually lies between p_h and p_f, and if in the absence of trade both countries produce both goods, $p_h < OD$ and $p_f > OA$, which in turn means that $OD > p^* > OA$.† Otherwise, p^* can lie anywhere between OD and OA, because p_h can lie anywhere between C and D, and p_f can be anywhere between A and B.

It is a simple matter to observe now that free trade could easily lead one country to complete specialisation. For example, suppose p^* equals OC, then under free trade, ω in H equals OR, so that H will be specialised in the first good. This would also happen if p^* came to lie anywhere between A and C. On the other hand, if p^* came to rest anywhere between B and D, the foreign country would get completely specialised in X_2 production. It is only if p^* lies in the

---

† If one country is very large in relation to the other, such that the introduction of international trade hardly creates a ripple in its economy, then its autarky commodity-price ratio is unaltered. The free-trade price ratio for the small country is then, of course, identical to the autarky commodity-price ratio of the large country. Realistically speaking, however, in a two-country model, both countries are large in relation to each other, so that the relative prices of both country's exportable goods rise, as each country in the presence of trade has to satisfy the domestic demand as well as the other country's demand for its export. Thus, with the home country exporting the first good, and the foreign country the second, the relative price of the first good rises in country H, so that p declines, whereas in country F the relative price of the second good rises, so that p rises. In the free trade equilibrium, only one price ratio prevails in both countries. It is clear from this analysis, then, that when the home country exports the first good and imports the second, $p_h > p^* > p_f$.

range BC that no country would be completely specialised in free trade.

Thus, the likelihood of complete specialisation by any country depends on the length of the overlapping-range BC; the latter in turn is determined, among other things, by how far apart are the overall capital/labour ratios of the two countries. Therefore, the likelihood of complete specialisation varies positively with the extent of the difference between k_h and k_f. Indeed, if there is no overlapping of the variation-range of the two countries' autarky price ratios, then under free trade, at least one country must get completely specialised in exportables. Thus, the possibility of specialisation decreases as the overlapping-range BC increases.

We will now show that this range of overlap rises in the presence of risk-averse behaviour. Under the latter proviso, we know that the ω–p relationship in the capital-abundant home country is depicted by a curve, such as HH', that lies above curve FF', which continues to represent the production structure in the foreign country. With HH', the variation-range of p in the home country at the original $k_h = O\bar{k}_h$ is given by EF, which means that overlapping-range of the two countries' autarky price ratios rises from BC to BE. In other words, in the presence of non-increasing absolute risk-aversion, the likelihood of complete specialisation by any country under free trade declines.

Finally, note that this result does not depend upon whether the good facing uncertainty is capital- or labour-intensive. Figure 4.7 is drawn on the basis of $k_1 < k_2$, and EF, the overlapping-range in the presence of uncertainty, exceeds BC, the corresponding range in the certainty case, thereby confirming our result.

4.5 Uncertainty and the Factor-Price Equalisation Theorem
One remarkable property of the deterministic H.O. model is that under certain conditions factor prices in the free trade equilibrium get completely equalised in the trading countries. We will now show that factor prices in the two countries can never be equalised in our stochastic framework, provided X_1 producers are risk-averse.

Let us first look at the customary proof of the factor-price equalisation theorem in terms of Fig. 4.8, where FF' depicts the ω–p relationship in both countries, when production conditions are non-stochastic. The free trade equilibrium price ratio is given by p^*, the ω corresponding to p^* is given by ω^* and is the same in both

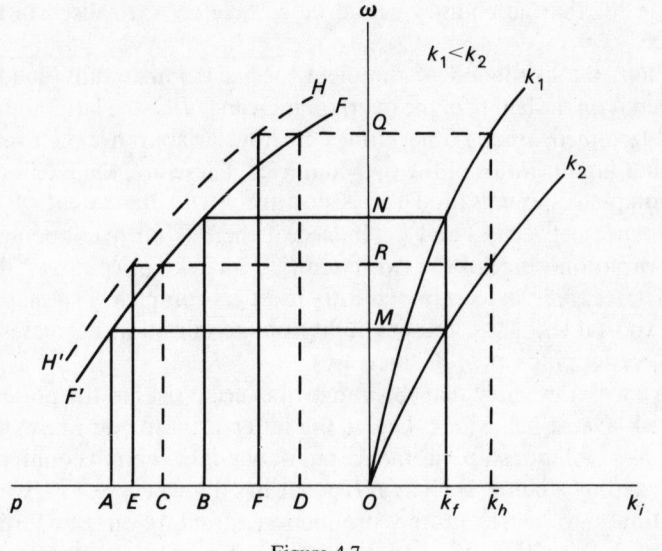

Figure 4.7

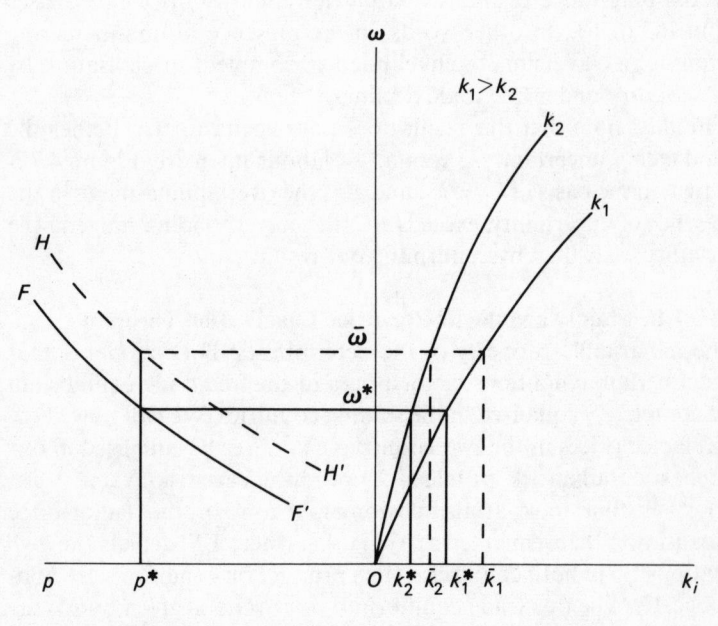

Figure 4.8

countries. Similarly, k_1 and k_2 at k_1^* and k_2^* are also the same in both countries. Since factor rewards in the deterministic case are determined by p, k_1 and k_2, and since the latter are identical in the two countries, the real factor rewards in free trade equilibrium must be identical in both countries.

A more visual demonstration of the factor-price equalisation theorem is provided by the following two equations which describe the factor market equilibrium in the certainty model:

$$w = f_1(k_1) - k_1 f_1'(k_1) = p[f_2(k_2) - k_2 f_2'(k_2)]$$

and

$$r = f_1'(k_1) = pf_2'(k_2).$$

Clearly then, if p, k_1 and k_2 are set at p^*, k_1^*, and k_2^* in both countries, w and r must be the same internationally.

One of the conditions necessary to ensure the factor-price equalisation theorem concerns the continued presence of incomplete specialisation in the free trade equilibrium, because otherwise the one-to-one relationship between p and ω, which is crucial to the validity of this theorem, does not hold. However, despite the improved likelihood of incomplete specialisation in the presence of risk-averse behaviour, factor rewards in our stochastic model do not get equalised internationally.

Let us revert to Fig. 4.8, where in the presence of risk-averse behaviour, the ω–p relationship for the capital-abundant home country is displayed by HH' and that for the foreign country by FF'. The variables with the asterisk are the free trade equilibrium variables for the foreign country, whereas the ones with the bar are the free trade variables prevailing in the home country. With $\bar{\omega} > \omega^*$, $\bar{k}_1 > k_1^*$ and $\bar{k}_2 > k_2^*$, it is clear that neither the relative nor the real factor rewards can get equalised in the two countries.

Until now, we have examined the implications of risk-averse behaviour for what may be called the 'strict' version of the factor-price equalisation theorem. There is a 'weak' version of the theorem, which, in recognition of the fact that complete equalisation of factor rewards in the trading countries is grossly unrealistic, merely suggests that factor rewards in the two countries become more proximate under free trade than before. How does this version fare in our stochastic framework?

It transpires that the weak version of the theorem continues to hold in our uncertainty model, provided that absolute risk-aversion is a non-increasing function of profits. Of course, in order for this to be true, all the assumptions sufficient to ensure the validity of the H.O. theorem must be satisfied. Once this is done, the argument suggests itself from the fact that, as established in Chapter 2, the Stolper–Samuelson theorem holds without any modification in spite of the presence of random elements in the economy.

For the sake of the argument, let us assume that the first sector is capital-intensive relative to the second at all factor prices. The capital-abundant home country then exports X_1 and imports X_2. The introduction of trade leads to a rise in the relative price of the first good for country H, and thus to a rise in the real reward of capital, which is used intensively by X_1, and a decline in the real reward of labour, a factor used unintensively by X_1. At the same time, the real reward of labour rises and that of capital declines in the foreign country. Given that the home country in the absence of trade also has a higher w and lower r than the foreign country, the exposure of the two economies to international trade must then bring inter-country factor rewards closer to each other.

Figure 4.9 explains what happens in each economy in its transition from no trade to free trade. This diagram consists of two boxes; one, with the supply of capital equal to O_1C and the supply of labour equal to O_1A, represents the structure of production in the capital-rich home country, and the other, with supply of capital and labour respectively equalling BO_2' and O_1B, portrays the economic structure in the labour-rich foreign country. The contract curve in each country is defined by the tangency of isoquants (not drawn) representing the actual outputs of X_1 (i.e. $\alpha^* F_1$) and the output of X_2.† The location of the two contract curves, $O_1 S_h P_h O_2$ and $O_1 P_f S_f O_2'$, reflects that $k_1 > k_2$ in both countries.

Let the autarky production and consumption points in H and F be respectively given by S_h and S_f. The introduction of trade results in a rise in the output of the exportable good in each country and a decline in the output of the importable good. Thus, X_1 rises in H with the supply of capital equal to O_1C and the supply of labour

† We introduced the concept of the expected contract curve in Chapter 2. Actually, the expected and the realised contract curves are essentially the same and both have identical characteristics, except that with the expected contract curve, the X_1 isoquants represent μF_1 and so on, whereas with the actual or the realised contract curve, the X_1 isoquants depict $\alpha^* F_1$, etc. In view of the linear homogeneity of the production functions, the switch from μ to α^* involves merely a renumbering of the X_1 isoquants.

and X_2 in F. On the other hand, X_2 declines in H and X_1 declines in F. In other words, the production point in H moves along its contract curve towards O_2, whereas the production point in F moves along its contract curve towards O_1, provided that firms are either risk-neutral or, if they are risk-averters, they have non-increasing absolute risk-aversion. The effect of international trade then is to bring the capital/labour ratios of the two industries closer to each

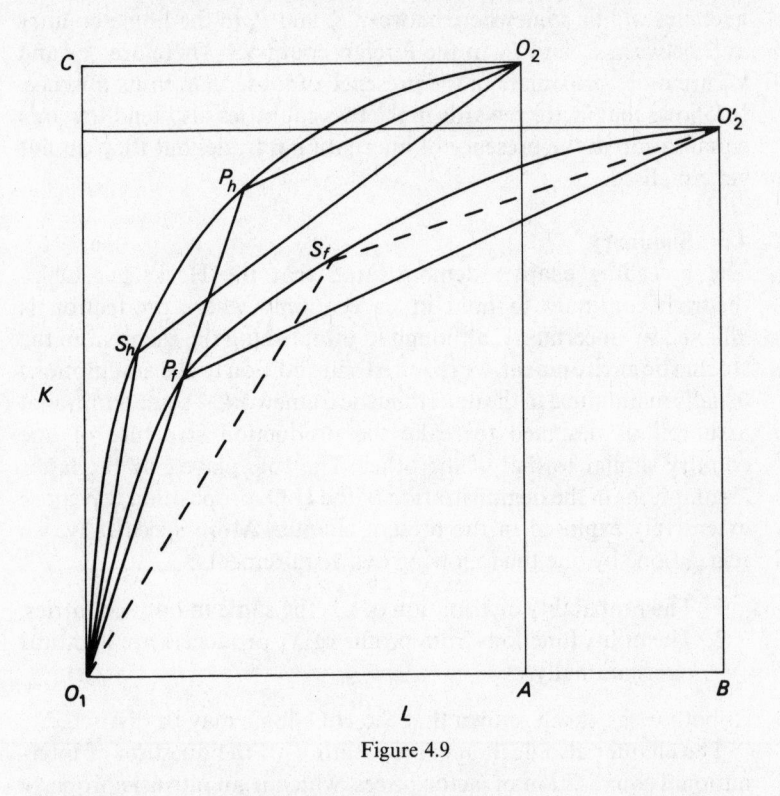

Figure 4.9

other internationally. Thus, k_{1h} comes closer to k_{1f} and k_{2h} to k_{2f}. In the limiting case of certainty or risk-neutrality, free trade results in

$$k_{1h} = k_{1f} \quad \text{and} \quad k_{2h} = k_{2f}.$$

In Fig. 4.9, in the free trade equilibrium under certainty, the production point is given by P_h in H and P_f in F, so that k_1 in both countries is given by the slope of $O_1 P_f P_h$, and k_2 by the slopes of $O_2 P_h$ and $O'_2 P_f$ which are parallel to each other. This is how, in the deterministic model, free trade results in the equality of k_1 and k_2 in both countries, and through this, the international equalisation of factor rewards.

In the presence of uncertainty and risk-averse behaviour, k_{ih} and k_{if} come closer to each other as a result of the introduction of trade, but they stop short of complete equalisation. The free trade production point in the presence of non-increasing absolute risk-aversion will lie somewhere between S_h and P_h in the home country and between S_f and P_f in the foreign country.† Therefore, k_{ih} and k_{if} are more proximate in the presence of trade than in its absence. It follows that factor rewards in the two countries also tend towards equalisation in the presence of international trade, but they do not get equalised.

4.6   Summary

The preceding chapter demonstrated that the Heckscher–Ohlin theorem continues to hold in an economy where production is afflicted by uncertainty, although in establishing the theorem in the stochastic environment, we required – in addition to the assumptions usually maintained in the deterministic framework—some additional assumptions designed to make the production structure of one country similar to that of the other. The role played by the latter assumptions in the demonstration of the H.O. proposition was more extensively explored in the present chapter. More specifically, we relaxed one by one the following two requirements:

1. The probability distribution of α is the same in both countries.
2. The utility functions from profits of X_1 producers are identical internationally.

In both cases, it was shown that the H.O. logic may be disrupted.

The chapter also dealt at some length with the question of international equalisation of factor prices, which is an intrinsic property of the deterministic H.O. model, provided the introduction of free trade does not lead any trading country to complete specialisation in the production of exportables. We discovered that in the presence of uncertainty and risk-averse behaviour, the likelihood of complete

† Since, in the presence of non-increasing absolute risk-aversion, the shift of the autarky production point in each country is smaller than that in the certainty case, risk-averse behaviour also contributes to a decline in the likelihood of complete specialisation consequent upon the introduction of international trade. This is, then, a further verification of the argument established in the preceding section.

specialisation consequent upon the introduction of trade diminishes, but despite this, factor prices in the trading countries do not get equalised, although, provided that the absolute risk-aversion is non-increasing, international trade does make them more proximate than does autarky. Thus, the weak version of the factor-price equalisation theorem continues to hold in the presence of non-increasing absolute risk-aversion.

REFERENCES

[1] Batra, R. N., *Studies in the Pure Theory of International Trade* (London: Macmillan, 1973).
[2] Hicks, J. R., *The Theory of Wages* (London: Macmillan, 1932).
[3] Johnson, H. G., *International Trade and Economic Growth* (Cambridge, Mass.: Harvard University Press, 1967) chap. 1.

5 The Heckscher–Ohlin Model Under Uncertainty: An Assessment

Owing to its simplicity and the plausibility of the results that it yields, the two-sector, two-factor, constant returns to scale framework, devised originally by Heckscher and Ohlin to develop a theory of the pattern of trade, has been extensively utilised in the exploration of various issues, some of which not even remotely resemble the question of the trade pattern. Nevertheless, irrespective of the context in which it is used, the two-sector model is generally called the H.O. model. Thus, although the Rybczynski, the Stolper–Samuelson and the factor-price equalisation theorems were discovered by different writers at different points in time, the structure of production underlying each proposition transpired to be the unifying H.O. model. In fact, it would not be inappropriate to say that the H.O. model has come to be identified with the two-by-two apparatus, whether or not the problem under consideration deals with international trade.†

In the last three chapters, an attempt has been made to integrate the customary, two-sector H.O. model with the analysis of economic behaviour under uncertainty. Ramifications of this integration are comprehensive and far-reaching. The present chapter is concerned with an assessment of the H.O. model under uncertainty. Does the presence of random elements cause irreparable damage to the attributes of the H.O. framework, or does it make any contribution towards enhancing its appeal, simply because the explicit consideration of uncertainty adds an extra dimension of realism to it?

On the basis of the analysis in the past three chapters, my general conclusion is that the introduction of uncertainty substantially increases the intuitive appeal of the H.O. model. Apart from certain factual considerations, the presence of risk-averse behaviour of pro-

---

† See, for example, Harberger [1] who describes his two-sector model of the incidence of corporation income-tax as the H.O. model.

ducers enables the H.O. model to get rid of some of its undesirable properties. For instance, the fact that with incomplete specialisation factor prices are related only to commodity prices and not at all to factor endowments and consequently the inevitable equalisation internationally of factor prices in free trade are some of the characteristics of the conventional H.O. model which are considered to be too restrictive.† In recognition of the glaring inequities in the living standards of trading countries, the reader may seriously doubt the application of the factor-price equalisation theorem to the real world.

Yet, there is some plausibility in the view that international trade ought to be instrumental in generating the proximity of factor rewards in the trading countries, because after all, economic systems are likely to be more different in autarky than with trade.‡ This desirable feature of an international trade model is preserved in the H.O. model in the presence of risk-averse behaviour, namely, that the reward of each factor in the two countries is closest (but not equal) in the presence of free trade.

This conclusion, of course, is intimately linked with the other property, characteristic only of the H.O. model under uncertainty, that factor prices are determined not only by commodity prices but also by factor supplies.

In addition to ridding the H.O. model of its undesirable properties, we have shown that in spite of uncertainty and the risk-averse behaviour of producers, the Heckscher–Ohlin explanation of the pattern of trade, the Rybczynski effect and the Stolper–Samuelson theorem continue to hold without any modification. Thus, our probabilistic reformulation of the two-sector model is not only based on more realistic considerations, but it also gets rid of the objectionable attritubes of the deterministic H.O. model, while preserving those properties which constitute the foundations of the modern theory of international trade.

Finally, all this is accomplished with the help of an innocuous assumption, namely, the absolute risk-aversion of the producers facing uncertainty is a non-increasing function of profits.

---

† See Jones [2, p. 3] for making a clear-cut statement to this effect.

‡ In this connection, it is perhaps pertinent to point out that Heckscher originally suggested that factor prices in his model had only a tendency towards equalisation. It is Samuelson [3] who, using the H.O. model, later provided a rigorous proof of the complete equalisation of factor rewards internationally.

REFERENCES

[1] Harberger, A. C., 'The Incidence of the Corporation Income Tax', *Journal of Political Economy*, 70 (June 1962) 215–40.

[2] Jones, R. W., 'A Three Factor Model in Theory, Trade and History', in J. N. Bhagwati *et al.* (eds.), *Trade, Balance of Payments and Growth* (Amsterdam: North Holland, 1971) chap. 1.

[3] Samuelson, P. A., 'International Factor Price Equalization Once Again', *Economic Journal*, 59 (June 1949) 181–97.

PART II Price Uncertainty

6 Economic Effects of Commodity-Price Stabilisation

Several underdeveloped countries complain that their developmental efforts are severely hampered by persistent and violent fluctuations in international prices of their export products and that this phenomenon causes instability in export earnings, and hence, in the availability of foreign exchange, which is so vital for growth. There is a plethora of economic literature, which deals with whether or not the export earnings of the underdeveloped nations are substantially more unstable than those of the developed nations, whether this instability is the result of oscillations in prices or in export supplies of primary products, whether countries facing higher fluctuations in export earnings grow at a slower rate than countries with relatively steady export earnings, and a whole host of related questions.†

In spite of the extensive literature, the theory of the economic consequences of vacillating export prices of underdeveloped nations is itself in a state of underdevelopment. Empirically, the economic effects of price instability have turned out to be inconclusive, whereas theoretically the analysis, whatever little is available, has concentrated on partial equilibrium techniques. For instance, in an empirical study, Coppock [2] concluded that the export earnings of less developed nations are only slightly more unstable than those of the developed nations, although the earnings instability of the former class of countries reflects violent movements in prices, whereas the instability for the richer nations stems primarily from fluctuations in export supplies.

One damaging repercussion of frequently vacillating prices, which has been largely overlooked, is that they create uncertainty in the economy and may thus have ramifications for the allocation of

† See, for example, the analyses by Caves and Jones [1, chap. 26], Kreinin [3, chap. 15] and Södersten [4, chap. 23], among many others.

resources. The existing literature recognises the uncertainty-generating potential of price oscillations and the consequential reluctance of underdeveloped economies to expand production of primary products for purposes of exports,† but, for lack of a proper general equilibrium framework, it fails to appreciate the fact that uncertainty caused by price variations can in general give rise to misallocation of resources, which can be rectified only by eliminating or minimising the cause of this instability, say, through international commodity agreements, which have been generally scoffed at as being ineffective or without much merit.

In this chapter, we show that the insistence of the underdeveloped nations on the formation of international commodity agreements (I.C.A.'s) is based on some solid economic reasons which have been hitherto missed by economists. It will be demonstrated that a reduction in uncertainty about prices in general leads (1) to a more efficient resource allocation and hence to a rise in national income, and (2) to a better distribution of income among labourers and the owners of capital.

The development of the chapter proceeds first with a brief review of the customary partial equilibrium arguments, which trumpet the inefficacy of the I.C.A.'s, and then with the construction of a general equilibrium model of price uncertainty along the lines of the production uncertainty framework presented in earlier chapters.

6.1 International Commodity Agreements

International trade in certain primary products is regulated by I.C.A.'s, which have been instituted primarily to stabilise export earnings from each commodity in question by stabilising its price. The nations pressing hard for these agreements argue that in some cases the price mechanism does not work efficiently, because the response of producers and consumers to price changes is awfully slow. This is, for instance, the case where the demand for a good is inelastic and the supply has a long gestation period, as is the case with many primary products. Thus, when the demand and supply curves for any product are inelastic, a small shift in either the demand or the supply curve causes disproportionately large changes in the equilibrium price. Therefore, some kind of price stabilising interven-

† See Caves and Jones [1, chap. 26] for further details.

tion in the free operation of market forces is required, and an I.C.A. constitutes an intervention of this type.

There are five I.C.A.'s which are currently operational. These concern agreements to regulate international trade in wheat, coffee, sugar, tin and powdered milk, while negotiations are taking place for several other agricultural products.

The I.C.A.'s instituted in the past have taken one of the following three forms:
1. Export-restriction schemes
2. Buffer stocks
3. Multilateral contracts

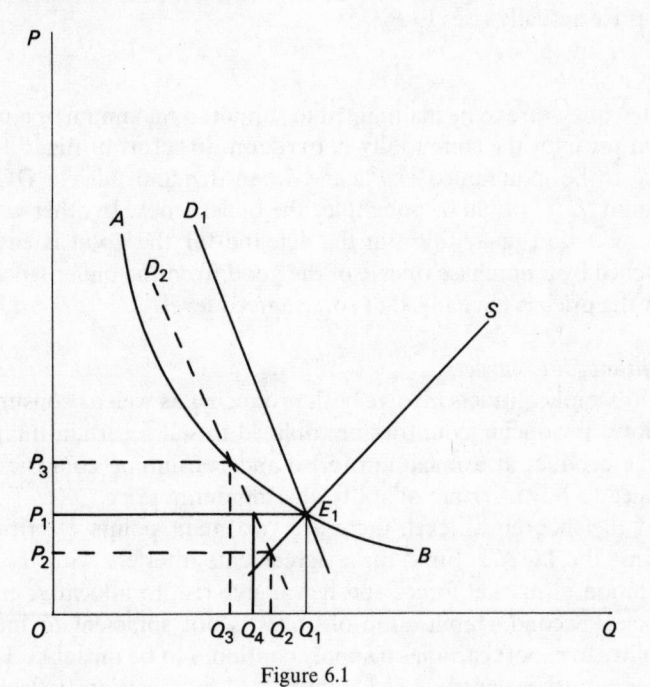

Figure 6.1

Export-Restriction Schemes
These schemes are designed to stabilise the export earnings by means of national quotas for the production or export of a particular commodity such that the total quantity marketed in the world can be manipulated in response to the demand conditions. The working of these schemes is described in Fig. 6.1, where the horizontal axis

measures the quantity exchanged, and the vertical axis measures the price of the product; AB is a rectangular hyperbola which has the property that the area or total earning underlying each point on the curve is the same; D_1 and S are the initial demand and supply curves, E_1 is the equilibrium point, and P_1 is the initial price, with the initial level of export earnings given by the area $OP_1E_1Q_1$. A temporary decline in demand shifts D_1 to D_2 and price in the absence of intervention would fall to P_2, and quantity marketed to Q_2. However, the export-restriction scheme would call for a greater reduction in supply through artificial withholding of the product. To maintain the original level of earnings, the supply should be reduced to Q_3 so that the price actually rises to P_3.

Buffer Stocks

Buffer stocks are to be maintained to support a maximum or a minimum price for the commodity in question. In terms of Fig. 6.1, the price to be maintained is P_1, and when demand falls to D_2, the amount Q_1Q_4 would be bought for the buffer stock. In other words, any reduction or addition in the demand for the good is equally matched by a purchase or sale of the good from the buffer stock, so that the price is unchanged at some agreed level.

Multilateral Contracts

Multilateral contracts involve both producing as well as consuming nations. Producing countries are obliged to sell a certain quantity of the product at a maximum price and consuming countries are obliged to buy a certain quantity at a minimum price.

At the theoretical level, there are two main points of criticism against the I.C.A.'s. First, these agreements interfere with the free operation of market forces and hence give rise to allocative inefficiencies. Second, stabilisation of prices is not sufficient to impart stability to export earnings if supply continues to be unstable. There are some other controversial points, too, but they are reflections more on the working of the I.C.A. rather than on the principle of price stabilisation.†

I believe that the allocative inefficiency aspect of regulating international prices has been in the past misconceived. When prices are stable, then, of course, the interference in the market mechanism

---

† See Södersten [4, chap. 23] for further details.

gives rise to allocative inefficiencies. But in a world where price vacillations generate uncertainty, price stabilisation will result in improved allocation of resources. This is what we demonstrate in the following in terms of a general equilibrium model. Even though price stability is not synonymous with steadiness of export earnings, our analysis yields rigorous theoretical arguments in favour of price-stabilisation policies *per se*.

6.2   A General Equilibrium Model of Production With Price Uncertainty

In the first part of this book, we introduced uncertainty in the economy by assuming that the production function in the first industry contained a random variable. This is, of course, not the only way through which the economic environment may become stochastic. As has been indicated in the preceding section, persistent and large movements in prices can also generate uncertainty in the economy. In this section, we modify the two-sector, general equilibrium model of production under uncertainty, utilised in the foregoing chapters, by assuming that the production functions are non-random but that X_1 producers face uncertain prices instead. As usual, the second industry is assumed to be free from uncertainty.

In order to blend this assumption suitably with the two-sector model under uncertainty, we have to introduce money in the economy. The deterministic two-sector models are the barter models where money plays no role. In our model, some conceptual problems arise if money is not present in the economy. In the barter model, all variables are measured in terms of any one good, and the results obtained are independent of which good is chosen as the unit of measurement. However, in a model where the price facing producers in one sector is uncertain, the results will depend on the particular good that serves as the numeraire. There is no problem if everything in the model is expressed in terms of the good with the non-random price. But if quantities are expressed in terms of the good facing the random price, then all prices, including the prices of factors, become random and the investigation of the problem may become anything but manageable. Thus, the results or perhaps the intelligibility of the price-uncertainty general equilibrium model will be sensitive to the choice of the numeraire.

In order to divest the model of this limiting feature, money may be explicitly introduced in the framework to serve merely as the unit of measurement. Thus, if all quantities are valued in terms of money, then p_2 may still be certain even if p_1 is a random variable, where p_i is the price of the ith good.

Note that this problem of the choice of the numeraire did not arise in the case where the production function in the first sector was assumed to be random, simply because p_1 was taken to be known with certainty, and it was possible to express quantities in terms of the price of any good without making all the prices random. In fact, the first good was chosen to be the numeraire.

The situation in which the price of only one good is random arises frequently in the regime of international trade. As suggested before, several underdeveloped countries find themselves in the unenviable position of exporting primary products at violently fluctuating and hence uncertain prices, while at the same time importing manufactured goods at reasonably steady prices. The question arises: Does this type of uncertainty have any influence on the economy's resource allocation, national income and income distribution? The assumptions of our analysis are made with a view to exploring this type of question, although in the author's view the model may have applicability to other areas of economics.

In addition, the following assumptions are maintained to facilitate our analysis.

1. All production functions are linearly homogeneous and concave. The producers of the first good are interested in maximising expected utility from profits and are risk-averse.
2. There is perfect competition in all markets, so that all producers are price-takers. This assumption with respect to the first sector implies that X_1 producers have no influence in the determination of the (subjective) distribution of p_1; in other words, X_1 producers are price-takers in the probabilistic sense.
3. The input–output decisions in the first sector are made before the knowledge of the actual price.
4. Full factor mobility in the long run, inelasticity of factor supplies and full employment are also assumed.
5. Finally, the country under question is a small country and by its action cannot influence the world terms of trade. In the context of our stochastic model, this implies that the price of the second good and the expected price of the first good are exogeneously given to the country.

Under these assumptions, the production side of the economy can be described by the following equations:

$$X_1 = F_1(K_1, L_1) = L_1 f_1(k_1) \tag{6.1}$$

$$X_2 = F_2(K_2, L_2) = L_2 f_2(k_2) \tag{6.2}$$

with $f_i' > 0$ and $f_i'' < 0$ $(i = 1, 2)$;

$$w = \frac{E[U'(\pi)p_1]}{E[U'(\pi)]}(f_1 - k_1 f_1') = p_2(f_2 - k_2 f_2') \tag{6.3*}$$

$$r = \frac{E[U'(\pi)p_1]}{E[U'(\pi)]} f_1' = p_2 f_2'. \tag{6.4*}$$

Without loss of generality, we assume that p_2 equals unity. Then from (6.3*) and (6.4*),

$$E[U'p_1](f_1 - k_1 f_1') = (f_2 - k_2 f_2')E[U'] \tag{6.3}$$

$$E[U'p_1]f_1' = f_2' E[U']. \tag{6.4}$$

With full employment

$$L_1 + L_2 = L \tag{6.5}$$

and

$$L_1 k_1 + L_2 k_2 = K. \tag{6.6}$$

Finally, the profit in the first industry is given by

$$\begin{aligned} \pi &= p_1 L_1 f_1 - wL_1 - rK_1 \\ &= L_1[p_1 f_1 - (f_2 - k_2 f_2') - k_1 f_2']. \end{aligned} \tag{6.7}$$

The reader may have noticed some differences between the present model and the one, developed in Chapter 2, concerning randomness in the production function of the first industry. There is no role for α in the present model, unless, of course, we are prepared to handle the complications arising in a two-random-variable model. To keep the analysis from exceeding the level of complexity already familiar to us, we will continue to confine our investigation to the single-random-variable model, but the random variable now is p_1 and not α. Since α is no longer a stochastic variable, we have chosen to delete it from the production function of the first industry. Otherwise, the analysis more or less remains the same. The factor market equilibrium conditions are derived in the same manner as first explained in Chapter 1 and then in Chapter 2. Full-employment equations, of course, remain unchanged, whereas the profit equation given by (6.7) changes to the extent that p_1 now supersedes α. Finally, note that w and r are now defined in money terms and not real terms.†

6.3   Price Stabilisation and Resource Allocation

Let us now examine the implications of price stabilisation on resource allocation in our two-sector economy. Since vacillating prices are the root cause of uncertainty in our model, the stabilisation of the international price of the first good (suppose X_1 is the primary product exported by the country in question) is inevitably accompanied by a decline in uncertainty, which, as explained in Chapter 1, can be defined in terms of the concept of the mean-preserving spread.

Let us define $\hat{p}_1$ as

$$\hat{p}_1 = \gamma p_1 + \theta$$

where γ and θ, as before, are the shift parameters. Then the decline in uncertainty is defined by

$$d\gamma < 0$$

along with

$$\frac{d\theta}{d\gamma} = -\mu_1 \tag{6.8}$$

† Although all quantities in the present model are expressed in money terms, the comparative-statics results derived below will be valid in real terms as well. For example, suppose all monetary variables are deflated by a general price index, P, which is some sort of a weighted index of the realised international price of the first good (p_1^*) and the price of the second good. That is,

$$P = \phi(p_1^*, p_2)$$

where the function ϕ is a linear homogeneous function of p_1^* and p_2. If p_1^* and p_2 are doubled, then P is also doubled, and so on. Furthermore,

$$\phi_1 = \frac{\partial \phi}{\partial p_1^*} > 0 \quad \text{and} \quad \phi_2 = \frac{\partial \phi}{\partial p_2} > 0.$$

If we assume that there is one unique set of realised international price of the first good and the price of the second good, then P is also uniquely determined.

Thus, if all the monetary variables are deflated by the general price index P, our comparative-statics results also hold in real terms. For example, suppose improved resource allocation leads to a rise in money national income for any internationally determined $E[p_1]$ and p_2. Then, since P is a unique number, especially for a small country which exercises no influence in determining either $E[p_1]$ or p_1^*, it is legitimate to say that the money national income deflated by P (which is the same thing as real income) also increases.

where μ_1 is the expected price of the first good, that is, μ_1 is the mean of the probability distribution of p_1.

Is there any prima facie case in favour of the argument that a change in the variance of p_1 alone (as represented by (6.8) and $d\gamma < 0$) generates repercussions for resource allocation in the entire economy, even though other things in the economy remain unaltered? The answer is in the affirmative. Because of competitive market conditions, atomistic firms in each sector act independently of what happens in the other sector. However, although in making their input–output decisions, competitive firms do not consider the effects of their actions on the other sectors, the combined impact of the actions of all firms in any sector reverberate throughout the economy. Thus, even though the change in the variance of p_1 does not affect the decision-making of X_2 producers, the effects of uncertainty on the decision-making of producers in the first sector generate repercussions which are felt in all other markets, including the markets for the second good and the two factors, capital and labour. This emerges vividly from the following analysis.

Differentiating the two full-employment equations, (6.5) and (6.6) with respect to γ, we obtain

$$\frac{\partial L_1}{\partial \gamma} = -\frac{\partial L_2}{\partial \gamma} = -\frac{1}{k_1 - k_2}\left[L_1\frac{\partial k_1}{\partial \gamma} + L_2\frac{\partial k_2}{\partial \gamma}\right]. \qquad (6.9)$$

Replacing p_1 in (6.3), (6.4) and (6.7) by $\hat{p}_1$, differentiating these equations with respect to γ, using (6.8) and evaluating the derivatives at $\theta = 0$ and $\gamma = 1$, we obtain the following system of equations:

$$\begin{bmatrix} A_1 & B_1 & C_1 \\ A_2 & B_2 & C_2 \\ (k_1 - k_2) & L_1 & L_2 \end{bmatrix} \begin{bmatrix} \partial L_1/\partial \gamma \\ \partial k_1/\partial \gamma \\ \partial k_2/\partial \gamma \end{bmatrix} = \begin{bmatrix} Q_1 \\ Q_2 \\ 0 \end{bmatrix} \qquad (6.10)$$

where
$$A_1/\omega = A_2 = E[U''h_1^2(k_1 + \omega)]$$
$$h_1 = p_1 F_{K1} - r$$
$$B_1 = E[\omega L_1 U''h_1^2 - k_1 f_1''U'p_1]$$
$$B_2 = E[L_1 U''h_1^2 + f_1''U'p_1] \qquad (6.11)$$
$$C_1 = E[\omega L_1 f_2''(k_2 - k_1)U''h_1 + k_2 f_2''U']$$
$$C_2 = E[L_1 f_2''(k_2 - k_1)U''h_1 - f_2''U']$$

and

$$Q_1/\omega = Q_2 = -E[(X_1 U''h_1 + F_{K1} U')(p_1 - \mu_1)].$$

The system of equations given by (6.10) includes (6.9). This system has been obtained in a manner discussed in the appendix to Chapter 2. As usual, the denominator, D, of the system (6.10) turns out to be positive under the hypothesis of non-increasing absolute risk-aversion.

The solution of (6.10) yields

$$\frac{\partial k_1}{\partial \gamma} = -\frac{f_2''(k_2 + \omega)E[U']Q_2(k_1 - k_2)}{D} \tag{6.12}$$

$$\frac{\partial k_2}{\partial \gamma} = -\frac{f_1''(k_1 + \omega)E[U'p_1]Q_2(k_1 - k_2)}{D} \tag{6.13}$$

$$\frac{\partial L_1}{\partial \gamma} = \frac{\{L_1 f_2''(k_2 + \omega)E[U'] + L_2 f_1''(k_1 + \omega)E[U'p_1]\}Q_2}{D}. \tag{6.14}$$

It can be observed from (6.14) that with $f_i'' < 0$ and $D > 0$, the sign of $\partial L_1/\partial \gamma$ depends on the sign of Q_2 which, from (6.11), is given by

$$Q_2 = -E[(X_1 U''h_1 + F_{K1} U')(p_1 - \mu_1)]$$

and, since X_1 and F_{K1} are non-random, Q_2 can be written as

$$Q_2 = -X_1 E[U''h_1(p_1 - \mu_1)] - F_{K1} E[U'(p_1 - \mu_1)]. \tag{6.15}$$

The sign of $E[U'(p_1 - \mu_1)]$ with risk-averse behaviour is negative because

$$E[U'(p_1 - \mu_1)] = E[U']E[p_1 - \mu_1] + \text{cov}[U', (p_1 - \mu_1)]$$

$$= \text{cov}[U', (p_1 - \mu_1)]$$

where the covariance between U' and $(p_1 - \mu_1)$ is negative, as

$$\text{sign cov}[U', (p_1 - \mu_1)] = \text{sign} \frac{\partial U'}{\partial \pi} \frac{\partial \pi}{\partial(p_1 - \mu_1)}$$

$$= \text{sign } U'' \frac{\partial \pi}{\partial(p_1 - \mu_1)}$$

and as $U'' < 0$ and $\partial \pi/\partial(p_1 - \mu_1) > 0$, $\text{cov}[U', (p_1 - \mu_1)] < 0$.

In the case of $E[U''h_1(p_1 - \mu_1)]$, we note that $E[U''h_1]$ can be shown to be non-negative in the presence of non-increasing absolute risk-aversion, as was done with the production-uncertainty model

in the appendix to Chapter 2. Furthermore, suppose we assume that
the initial situation is one of certainty and that price is known to be
equal to the mean of its probability distribution. In this case, the
factor rewards initially are determined by the value of their marginal
products, so that with p_1 initially equal to μ_1, $w = \mu_1 F_{L1}$ and
$r = \mu_1 F_{K1}$, in which case

$$h_1 = p_1 F_{K1} - r = (p_1 - \mu_1)F_{K1}$$

so that

$$E[U''h_1(p_1 - \mu_1)] = E[U''(p_1 - \mu_1)^2]F_{K1}$$

is clearly negative for risk-averse firms. On the other hand, in the
more general case, where the initial situation is one of uncertainty,
we can write

$$E[U''h_1(p_1 - \mu_1)] = E\left[U''h_1\left(p_1 - \frac{r}{F_{K1}} + \frac{r}{F_{K1}} - \mu_1\right)\right]$$

$$= E\left[\frac{U''h_1^2}{F_{K1}}\right] + E[U''h_1]\frac{(r - \mu_1 F_{K1})}{F_{K1}}.$$

It can be easily shown that with risk-averse firms,

$$r \leqslant \mu_1 F_{K1}.$$

With non-increasing absolute risk-aversion ensuring that

$$E[U''h_1] \geqslant 0,$$

it is clear that

$$E[U''h_1(p_1 - \mu_1)] < 0.$$

Thus, we conclude that $E[U''h_1(p_1 - \mu_1)]$ is negative, if firms in
sector 1 are risk-averse and initially price is known with certainty
to be equal to the mean of the probability distribution, or X_1
firms have non-increasing absolute risk-aversion functions. It is
now a simple matter to observe that these two conditions are also
sufficient to ensure that Q_2 from (6.15) is positive.

With $Q_2 > 0$, $\partial L_1/\partial \gamma$ from (6.14) is clearly negative. The sign of
$\partial K_1/\partial \gamma$ can be determined analogously, as

$$\frac{\partial K_1}{\partial \gamma} = L_1 \frac{\partial k_1}{\partial \gamma} + k_1 \frac{\partial L_1}{\partial \gamma}$$

which, in view of (6.12) and (6.14), becomes

$$\frac{\partial K_1}{\partial \gamma} = \frac{\{L_1 k_2 (k_2 + \omega) f_2'' E[U'] + k_1 L_2 f_1'' (k_1 + \omega) E[U' p_1]\} Q_2}{D}.$$

With $Q_2 > 0$, $\partial K_1 / \partial \gamma$ is clearly negative. With inelastic factor supplies then, $\partial K_2 / \partial \gamma$ and $\partial L_2 / \partial \gamma$ must be positive. The following theorem can be derived immediately:

Theorem 6.1. A decline in uncertainty ($d\gamma < 0$) arising from the stabilisation of prices stimulates the movement of resources from the certainty industry to the industry facing uncertainty, provided the absolute risk-aversion is a non-increasing function of profits, and conversely.

This theorem, of course, becomes irrelevant when the initial situation is one of certainty, because then, speaking of a change in uncertainty makes little sense. But the discussion so far in this section yields an additional result which is condensed in theorem 6.2.

Theorem 6.2. The introduction of uncertainty causes resources to move away from the industry facing uncertainty to the industry operating under certainty.

With these two theorems at hand, it is a simple matter now to deduce that the introduction of uncertainty or an increase in uncertainty about p_1 leads to a decline in the output of X_1 and a rise in the output of X_2.

6.4 Price Stabilisation and Income Distribution

The implications of the stabilisation of prices for factor rewards, and hence income distribution, are closely related to the way uncertainty affects the capital/labour ratio in each industry. Equations (6.12) and (6.13) facilitate our exposition in this connection. The conditions which impart Q_2 a determinate, positive sign have already been obtained. Equations (6.12) and (6.13) then clearly suggest that, given these conditions, the sign of $\partial k_1 / \partial \gamma$ and $\partial k_2 / \partial \gamma$ is the same as the sign of $(k_1 - k_2)$. This follows from the fact that $f_i'' < 0$ and $D > 0$. Therefore, an increase in γ and hence in the variance of p_1 alone, contributes to a rise in the capital/labour ratio in both industries, if the industry facing uncertainty is capital-intensive relative to the certainty industry, and to a decline in the capital/labour ratio in both industries if the first sector is labour-intensive relative to the second. These results are reversed for the case of a decline in the variance of p_1 alone.

Since the capital/labour ratios in both industries move unidirectionally in response to the change in the variance, there is an unambiguous movement in factor prices, which are determined by product prices and marginal factor productivities and hence by the capital/labour ratio in each industry.† Thus, if both k_1 and k_2 rise, then with given p_2 and μ_1, the wage-rate would rise and the rental-rate decline in both industries, and conversely for the case of a decline in both k_1 and k_2.

These results become visually clear if we differentiate the equations

$$w = p_2(f_2 - k_2 f_2')$$

and

$$r = p_2 f_2'$$

to obtain (with $p_2 = 1$ initially)

$$\frac{\partial w}{\partial \gamma} = -k_2 f_2'' \frac{\partial k_2}{\partial \gamma}$$

and

$$\frac{\partial r}{\partial \gamma} = f_2'' \frac{\partial k_2}{\partial \gamma}.$$

With $f_2'' < 0$, it is evident that the sign of $\partial w/\partial \gamma$ is similar whereas the sign of $\partial r/\partial \gamma$ is opposite to the sign of $\partial k_2/\partial \gamma$. The following theorem is then immediate:

Theorem 6.3. An increase in uncertainty stimulates a decline in the reward of the factor used intensively by the industry facing uncertainty, and a rise in the reward of the factor used intensively by the industry operating under certainty, provided the absolute risk-aversion is non-increasing in profits, and conversely.

Needless to say, the introduction of uncertainty also leads to the results obtained in theorem 6.3, if the X_1 firms are risk-averters.

The proof of these results derives from the fact that in view of (6.12) and (6.13),

† Perhaps, it is more accurate to say that the product price and the marginal productivity of factors in the second sector only determine the factor rewards.

$$\frac{\partial w}{\partial \gamma} \gtrless 0 \quad \text{if} \quad k_1 \gtrless k_2$$

and

$$\frac{\partial r}{\partial \gamma} \lessgtr 0 \quad \text{if} \quad k_1 \gtrless k_2.$$

A geometrical illustration of theorems 6.1–6.3 turns out to be highly rewarding in terms of clarity and comprehension. Consider Fig. 6.2, where factor supplies are measured along the two axes, and

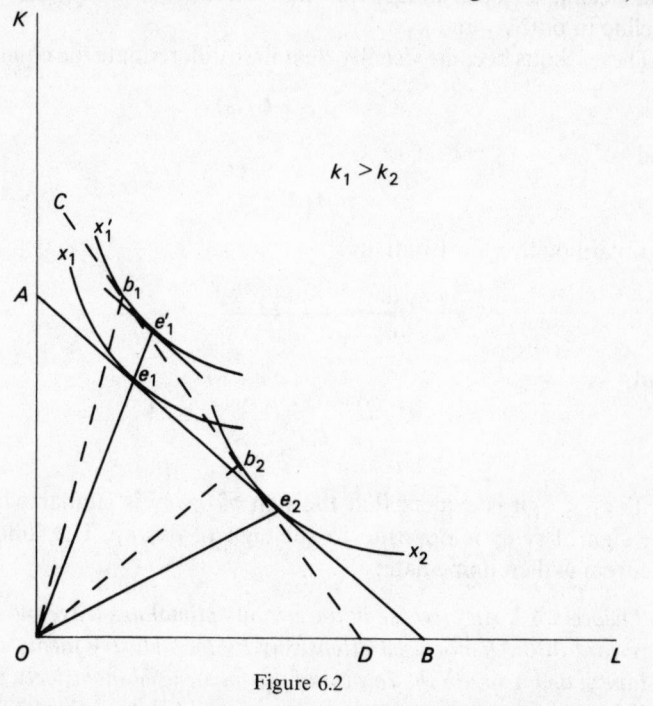

Figure 6.2

x_1 and x_2 are the unit isoquants of the first and the second industry respectively. If the initial situation is one of certainty, then the isocost line is given by AB, with points e_1 and e_2 determining the equilibrium capital/labour ratio in each industry. As suggested in Chapter 1, the presence of uncertainty and risk-averse behaviour can be represented by an outward neutral shift of the unit isoquant x_1 to x_1', such that, at the original wage/rental ratio, the capital/labour ratio remains the same, but the output of X_1 declines below unity to Oe_1/Oe_1'.

Suppose in the certainty situation $p_1 = \mu_1$. Then initially, since the two unit isoquants lie on the same isocost line, p_2/μ_1 equals unity. The only way to maintain this original ratio p_2/μ_1 in the presence of risk-averse behaviour is to draw a tangent common to the new X_1 unit isoquant, x_1', and the original X_2 unit isoquant, x_2. This new common tangent is given by CD, which shows that the wage/rental ratio rises, and so does the capital/labour ratio in each industry, as the equilibrium points shift to b_1 and b_2. This occurs in Fig. 6.2 because the diagram is based on the assumption that $k_1 > k_2$. In Fig. 6.3, where $k_1 < k_2$, the introduction of uncertainty

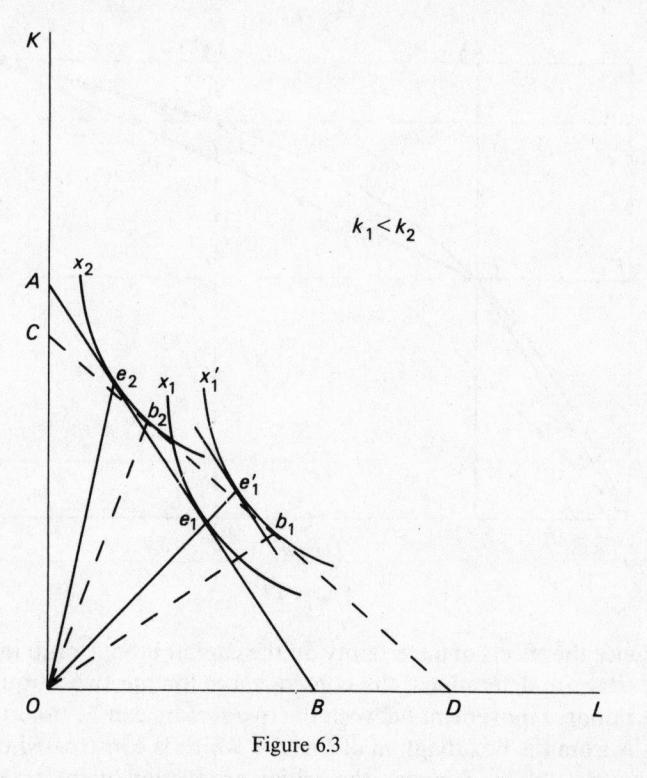

Figure 6.3

promotes a decline in the capital/labour ratio in each industry.

It can also be seen intuitively that an increase in the variance alone, with μ_1 constant, can be represented by a further outward and neutral shift of the X_1 unit isoquant, provided, of course, that absolute risk-aversion is non-increasing. Owing to risk-aversion, X_1

producers produce a lower output at the original factor prices than would be the case if the price were known with certainty to be equal to μ_1. It seems natural then, that an increase in the variance would lead to a further decline in the output at the original factor prices and μ_1, but only if it enhances the firms' aversion towards risk, which is possible only if the absolute risk-aversion is a non-increasing function of profits. In other words, under the latter proviso, an increase in the variance, alone, can be represented by a neutral shift of the unit isoquant away from the origin.

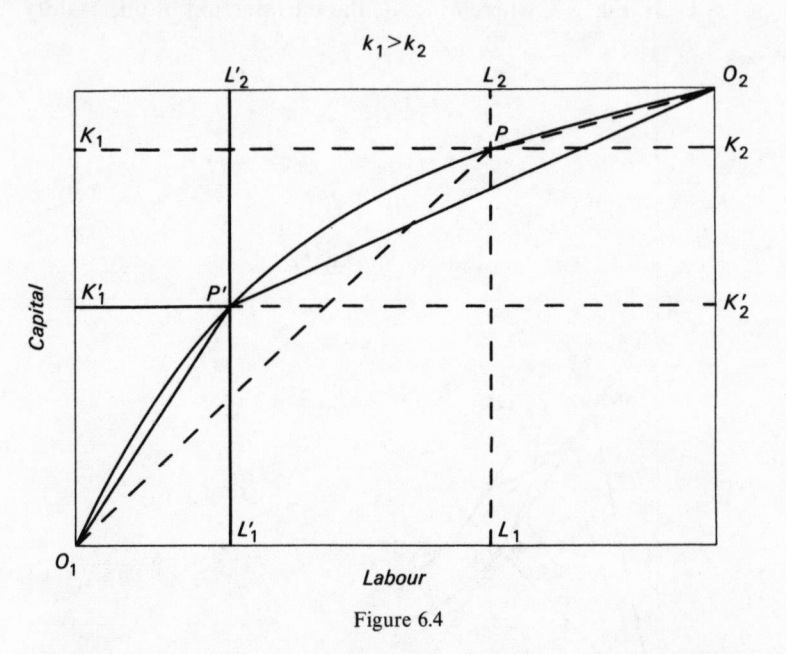

Figure 6.4

Once the effects of uncertainty on the capital/labour ratio in each industry are determined, the consequences for the two outputs or the resource movement between the two sectors can be ascertained easily from the box diagram of Fig. 6.4, which is constructed on the basis of $k_1 > k_2$. Suppose the initial production point is P, the amounts of labour and capital employed in the first sector are O_1L_1 and O_1K_1, whereas the corresponding amounts in the second sector are O_2L_2 and O_2K_2. The introduction of uncertainty or a marginal increase in uncertainty in X_1 promotes a rise in the capital/labour ratios in X_1 and X_2 from the initial slopes of O_1P and O_2P respectively, to those of O_1P' and O_2P'; the employment of labour and capital declines in X_1 respectively, to $O_1L'_1$ and $O_1K'_1$ but rises in X_2 to $O_2L'_2$ and $O_2K'_2$. Thus, the output of the first industry declines and that of the second industry rises. Similar results can be obtained in the case where $k_1 < k_2$.

6.5 Price Stabilisation and National Income

Once it is established that a change in uncertainty about p_1 gives rise to the movement of resources from one industry to the other, it is evident at first blush that the change in the variance will also have repercussions for expected national income, Y, which is defined as

$$Y = p_1 X_1 + p_2 X_2$$

or

$$E[Y] = \bar{Y} = E[p_1]X_1 + p_2 X_2 = \mu_1 X_1 + p_2 X_2. \qquad (6.16)$$

In order to investigate the effects of uncertainty on national income, we need the expression for the marginal rate of transformation in equilibrium. Following the method developed in Chapter 2, it can be shown that

$$\frac{dX_1}{dX_2} = -\frac{p_2 E[U']}{\mu_1 E[U'] + \text{cov}(U', p_1)} = -\beta \frac{p_2}{\mu_1} \qquad (6.17)$$

where

$$\beta = \frac{E[U']\mu_1}{E[U']\mu_1 + \text{cov}(U', p_1)}. \qquad (6.18)$$

With $\text{cov}(U', p_1) < 0$ in the presence of risk-averse behaviour, $\beta > 1$.

Let us now compare the level of national income under uncertainty with that attainable under certainty. There is no obvious way of making this comparison because under certainty,

$$\frac{dX_1}{dX_2} = -\frac{p_2}{p_1}$$

whereas under uncertainty,

$$\frac{dX_1}{dX_2} = -\beta \frac{p_2}{\mu_1}$$

where β is defined above. But there is one intuitively appealing way of formulating the problem: What is the level of national income under uncertainty as compared to the case where p_1 is known with certainty to be equal to the mean of the original distribution?

The Pareto optimality condition for national-income maximisation is that the marginal rate of transformation be equal to the negative of the given international-price ratio. With $p_1 = \mu_1$, this means that

$$\frac{dX_1}{dX_2} = -\frac{p_2}{\mu_1}. \tag{6.19}$$

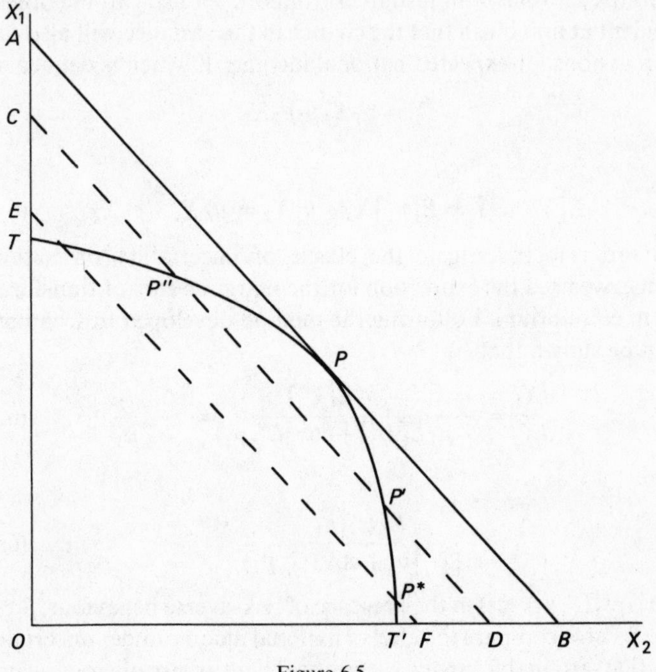

Figure 6.5

Under perfect competition in all markets, condition (6.19) is indeed satisfied under certainty conditions, and the national income is at the maximum.

In the presence of uncertainty, (6.19) will be satisfied only if the X_1 firms are risk-neutral because then, β from (6.18) equals one. However, if the firms are risk-averters (or even risk-preferers), (6.19) is violated, so that national income under certainty is higher than the income under uncertainty.

A geometrical illustration of this result is provided by Fig. 6.5, where TT' is the transformation curve, and the slope of AB, parallel to CD, reflects the internationally determined level of p_2/μ_1. Under certainty conditions or with risk-neutrality, the production point is given by P, whereas with risk-aversion, the production point is P' and in the risk-preference case, the production point is P''. Since CD lies below AB, *national income under certainty is higher than national income under uncertainty, given that firms are in general risk-averse.*

Next we analyse the implications of a marginal change in uncertainty for expected national income. Let us replace p_1 by $\hat{p}_1$ in (6.16) to obtain

$$\bar{Y} = E[\gamma p_1 + \theta]X_1 + p_2 X_2.$$

Differentiating this with respect to γ, equating $d\theta/d\gamma$ to $-\mu_1$, and remembering that initially $\theta = 0$ and $\gamma = 1$ and that p_2 is given, we obtain

$$\frac{d\bar{Y}}{d\gamma} = \mu_1 \frac{dX_1}{d\gamma} + X_1 E[p_1 - \mu_1] + p_2 \frac{dX_2}{d\gamma}$$

$$= \frac{dX_2}{d\gamma}\left[\mu_1 \frac{dX_1}{dX_2} + p_2\right]$$

Substituting from (6.17), we have

$$\frac{d\bar{Y}}{d\gamma} = p_2 \frac{dX_2}{d\gamma}[1 - \beta] \tag{6.20}$$

where, as before,

$$\beta = \frac{E[U']\mu_1}{E[U']\mu_1 + \mathrm{cov}\,(U', p_1)}.$$

Since with risk-averse firms, $\beta > 1$, it is clear that the sign of $d\bar{Y}/d\gamma$ depends on the sign of $dX_2/d\gamma$, which in section 6.3 was shown to be positive in the presence of non-increasing absolute risk-aversion. The following theorem is then clearly available:

Theorem 6.4. An increase in uncertainty contributes to a decline in expected national income in the presence of non-increasing absolute risk-aversion, and vice versa.

The theorem follows from the fact that with $dX_2/d\gamma > 0$, $d\bar{Y}/d\gamma < 0$ because $\beta > 1$.

Reverting to Fig. 6.5, suppose the initial production point under

E

the risk-averse behaviour is P'. If a rise in the variance of the distribution of p_1 is not accompanied by a change in its mean, then the original level of p_2/μ_1 remains unaltered, but the production point moves along TT' towards T' to reflect the decline in the output of X_1 and a rise in the output of X_2 provided absolute risk-aversion is non-increasing. Suppose the new production point is P^* and the new price line is EF. Since EF lies below CD, an increase in uncertainty has generated a decline in expected national income. Similarly, it can be shown that a decline in uncertainty contributes to a rise in expected national income.

6.6 Arguments in Favour of Price Stabilisation

The theorems developed in this chapter enable us to present some arguments which favour the pursuit by underdeveloped countries of international trade policies designed to stabilise the prices of primary products.

The most potent argument for the stabilisation of the international prices of primary products springs from theorem 6.4, because in so far as price stabilisation contributes to a decline in uncertainty, resource allocation becomes more efficient and the expected national income rises. This also vividly demonstrates the speciousness of the customary argument that the international regulation of primary products gives rise to allocative inefficiencies.† If anything, the allocative efficiency in the economy improves.

The second argument for steady prices is provided by theorem 6.3, which suggests that a decline in uncertainty contributes to a rise in the reward of the factor used intensively by the industry facing uncertainty and to a decline in the reward of the other factor. In most underdeveloped countries, primary producing industries are labour-intensive relative to import-competing manufactured goods. It follows then, that the price-stabilisation policy will promote a rise in the reward of labour and a decline in the reward of capital and, to this extent, lead to a socially more acceptable distribution of income. Thus, price-stabilisation policies benefit workers at the expense of the owners of capital. All that is needed to ensure these effects is that the absolute risk-aversion is non-increasing in profits.

† See Kreinin [3, p. 288] for an expression of the prevailing view.

6.7 Summary

In this chapter, we developed a two-sector, two-factor, general equilibrium model of a small country which takes international prices as given. In the case of the good with fluctuating, and hence, uncertain international prices, the small-country assumption means that the *expected* price of this good is exogeneously given. The country in question, or more appropriately, its residents, have then no say in the determination of the probability distribution of the international price. Thus, the small country is a price-taker in the probabilistic sense.

The general equilibrium model of price uncertainty was utilised to develop some arguments in favour of the policies of price stabilisation, which may be regarded as synonymous with a decline in uncertainty. We showed, among other things, that the price-stabilisation policies of an underdeveloped country result in (1) a rise in the output of the primary product, (2) a shift in the distribution of income in favour of labour and against capital, and (3) a rise in expected national income.

REFERENCES

[1] Caves, R. E., and Jones, R. W., *World Trade and Payments: An Introduction* (Boston: Little, Brown, 1973) chap. 26.

[2] Coppock, J. D., *International Economic Instability; The Experience After World War II* (New York: McGraw-Hill, 1972) chap. 4.

[3] Kreinin, M. E., *International Economics: A Policy Approach* (New York: Harcourt Brace Jovanovich, 1971) chap. 15.

[4] Södersten, Bo, *International Economics* (New York: Harper and Row, 1970) chap. 23.

7   Gains From Trade
Under Uncertainty

No treatise on the theory of international trade can be considered complete without some discussion of the subject of the gains from trade. Accordingly, this chapter is devoted to a dissection of the anatomy of gains from trade in a stochastic environment. In other words, unlike the earlier chapters which were primarily concerned with positive aspects of trade theory under uncertainty, the present chapter will deal with the welfare or normative aspects of international trade, although it would be fair to say that some sections of the foregoing chapters did investigate the normative aspects as well. The study of the implications of commodity-price-stabilisation policies for the allocative efficiency of the economic system, after all, does have some welfare connotations.

What we showed in the last chapter was that (1) national income under uncertainty is lower than the certainty level of income, provided that firms are not risk-neutral, and (2) an increase in uncertainty culminates in a decline in expected national income, provided the absolute risk-aversion of the firms is non-increasing in profits. In this chapter, we extend the price-uncertainty apparatus of the preceding chapter to include the social-utility function of the consumers as well. The full dissection of the gains from trade proceeds in three steps. First, the effects of uncertainty on national income under the risk-averse behaviour of producers are examined, a task that has already been accomplished in the previous chapter; second, we explore the implications of the stochastic environment for social utility by assuming that producers are risk-apathetic, but the consumers are risk-averse; finally, the effects of uncertainty for social welfare are explored in the case where both producers and consumers evince aversion towards risk.

An interesting feature of our formulation is that some results turn out to be sensitive to whether or not the industry facing uncertain world prices is an import-competing industry or the one producing the exportable good. It is worth noting in this connection that so far as underdeveloped countries are concerned, the good facing price uncertainty is the exportable good. But this only means that for developed countries trading with the less developed ones, the good facing uncertainty is the import-competing good. In the interest of generality, therefore, both cases should be diagnosed.

7.1 The Formal Model

As in the previous chapter, we assume that the country under consideration is a small country and is a price-taker in the stochastic sense; the price of the second good is known with certainty and the country's beliefs about the price of the first good can be summarised in a subjective probability distribution.

In this section, we assume that producers are risk-neutral but the consumers are risk-averters. The social utility of the community is represented by a social-welfare function, such as

$$W = W(C_1, C_2) \tag{7.1}$$

where W is welfare and C_i denotes the consumption of the ith good ($i = 1, 2$). The postulation of a social-welfare function enables us to ignore the problem of income distribution because the latter becomes inherent in the choice of the utility index. There is no satiation in consumption, and the marginal utility of each good, denoted by $W_i = \partial W / \partial C_i$, is positive but decreasing so that $W_i > 0$ and $W_{ii} = \partial^2 W / \partial C_i^2 < 0$. Furthermore, we assume that $W_{ij} > 0$ ($i, j = 1, 2; i \neq j$).

Given these assumptions and the framework of the foregoing chapter, the problem can be formulated in this way. Producers maximise expected utility from profits, and their production, constrained by the given factor supplies, determines the level of national income given by

$$Y = p_1 X_1 + p_2 X_2. \tag{7.2}$$

Consumers then maximise utility subject to their budget constraint which restricts the value of their consumption to the value of the economy's production, that is,

$$p_1 C_1 + p_2 C_2 = p_1 X_1 + p_2 X_2 = Y. \tag{7.3}$$

It was shown in the preceding chapter that the producers' decision-making under uncertainty resulted in the following equation:

$$\frac{dX_1}{dX_2} = -\beta \frac{p_2}{\mu_1} \tag{7.4}$$

where, as before, μ_1 is the expected price of the first good, and

$$\beta = \frac{\mu_1 E[U']}{\mu_1 E[U'] + \text{cov}(U', p_1)} \tag{7.5}$$

with $\beta = 1$ under the risk-neutrality of X_1 producers.

As regards consumers (or the representative consumer), the social-welfare function itself is non-random, but randomness enters into the welfare function when we substitute for C_2, from (7.3) in (7.1), to obtain

$$W = W\left(C_1, \frac{p_1}{p_2}X_1 + X_2 - \frac{p_1}{p_2}C_1\right).$$

Therefore, the community maximises

$$E[W] = E\left[W\left(C_1, \frac{p_1}{p_2}X_1 + X_2 - \frac{p_1}{p_2}C_1\right)\right] \tag{7.6}$$

by choosing C_1 before actual p_1 is known, thereby treating C_2 as a random variable.† The randomness of C_2, of course, stems from the randomness of p_1. Note that it makes little difference to the analysis if the consumers decided to choose C_2 before the resolution of p_1.

Differentiating (7.6) with respect to C_1, we obtain the necessary conditions for expected welfare maximisation:

$$\frac{dE[W]}{dC_1} = E\left[W_1 - \frac{p_1}{p_2}W_2\right] = 0 \tag{7.7}$$

and

$$\frac{d^2 E[W]}{dC_1^2} = E\left[W_{11} + W_{12}\frac{dC_2}{dC_1} - \frac{p_1}{p_2}\left(W_{21} + W_{22}\frac{dC_2}{dC_1}\right)\right] < 0. \tag{7.8}$$

---

† It is interesting to note that our formulation is relevant to the planning problem in several underdeveloped countries. As stated in the preceding chapter, many of these countries face uncertainty about their terms of trade either because of past fluctuations in world prices or because of the nature of the goods they export. Quite often, the central planners or the architects of commercial policy seek to fulfil certain export targets before the knowledge of actual world prices, either in order to alleviate the critical foreign exchange shortage or in order to obtain capital goods from abroad for investment. However, setting the export target in advance of the resolution of the terms of trade is equivalent to choosing the level of C_1 for the community, because the optimal output of X_1 is determined by the producers.

In the derivation of (7.7) and (7.8), we have assumed that X_1 and X_2 are not affected by the level of C_1 chosen, because the output levels are determined by producers independent of the consumers' choice.

Since from (7.3),

$$\frac{dC_2}{dC_1} = -\frac{p_1}{p_2}$$

equation (7.8) becomes

$$\frac{d^2 E[W]}{dC_1^2} = E[W_{11} + (p_1/p_2)^2 W_{22} - 2p_1 W_{12}/p_2] < 0. \qquad (7.9)$$

Equation (7.9) furnishes the second-order condition for expected welfare maximisation. From our assumptions that $W_{ii} < 0$ and $W_{ij} > 0$, it is clear that consumers will infact be able to achieve the maximum.

Let us investigate at some length the properties of the first-order condition for expected welfare maximisation. From (7.7),

$$E[W_1] = E[p_1 W_2/p_2]. \qquad (7.10)$$

In order to obtain further information from (7.10), it is necessary to specify how W_2 and p_1 are related. If we assume that consumers are risk-neutral, the problem is considerably simplified because then $W_{22} = 0$ and

$$E[p_1 W_2] = E[p_1]E[W_2] = \mu_1 E[W_2]$$

so that (7.10) becomes

$$\frac{E[W_1]}{E[W_2]} = \frac{\mu_1}{p_2}.$$

In this case, the consumers maximise expected welfare by equating what may be called the expected international-price ratio (μ_1/p_2) to the ratio of expected marginal utilities or the marginal rate of expected substitution.

In general, however, $W_{22} < 0$ and W_2 and p_1 are correlated. Furthermore, this correlation depends on whether the first good is imported or exported in equilibrium. This is shown as follows:

The expected consumption of C_2 from (7.3) is given by

$$p_2 E[C_2] = p_2 \bar{C}_2 = \mu_1 (X_1 - C_1) + p_2 X_2.$$

Substituting for X_2 in (7.3) furnishes

$$p_2 C_2 = p_2 \bar{C}_2 + (X_1 - C_1)(p_1 - \mu_1). \tag{7.11}$$

Without loss of generality, we assume hereafter that $p_2 = 1$. It is clear from (7.11) that two cases can be distinguished, depending on whether $X_1 \gtrless C_1$.

$$\text{If } X_1 > C_1, \; C_2 \gtrless \bar{C}_2 \qquad \text{for } p_1 \gtrless \mu_1 \tag{i}$$

and

$$\text{if } X_1 < C_1, \; C_2 \lessgtr \bar{C}_2 \qquad \text{for } p_1 \gtrless \mu_1. \tag{ii}$$

Since C_1 is chosen by the community before knowledge of p_1, and since X_1 and X_2 are determined by producers independent of consumers' actions, the two random variables left in the budget constraint (7.3) are C_2 and p_1, with p_1 being the independent, and C_2 the dependent, random variable. Now the marginal utility from the consumption of each good is normally a function of both C_1 and C_2, but since C_1 is chosen in advance, W_i is responsive only to the levels of C_2, provided, of course, the parameters of the economic system remain unchanged. Thus, we may write

$$W_2 = W_2(C_2)$$

with $W_{22} < 0$ in the general case of risk-aversion.

Consider now the case where $X_1 > C_1$ so that the country chooses the production and consumption of the first good in such a way that it is exported in the free trade equilibrium. In this case

$$C_2 \gtrless \bar{C}_2 \qquad \text{for } p_1 \gtrless \mu_1.$$

With $W_{22} < 0$, it means that

$$W_2(C_2) \lessgtr W_2(\bar{C}_2) \qquad \text{for } p_1 \gtrless \mu_1.$$

Multiplying both sides by $p_1 - \mu_1$, we obtain

$$W_2(C_2)(p_1 - \mu_1) \leqslant W_2(\bar{C}_2)(p_1 - \mu_1) \qquad \text{for all } p_1$$

or

$$E[W_2(C_2)(p_1 - \mu_1)] \leqslant W_2(\bar{C}_2)E[p_1 - \mu_1]$$

or

$$E[W_2(C_2)(p_1 - \mu_1)] \leqslant 0. \tag{7.12}$$

Similarly, if $X_1 < C_1$, it can be readily established that

$$E[W_2(C_2)(p_1 - \mu_1)] \geqslant 0. \tag{7.13}$$

However,

$$E[W_2(p_1 - \mu_1)] = E[W_2 p_1] - \mu_1 E[W_2] = \text{cov}(W_2, p_1). \tag{7.14}$$

Substituting $E[W_2 p_1]$ from (7.14) in (7.10) yields

$$\frac{E[W_1]}{E[W_2]} = \frac{\mu_1}{p_2} + \frac{\text{cov}(W_2, p_1)}{E[W_2]} \tag{7.15}$$

remembering that p_2 initially equals one.

So long as consumers are not indifferent to risk, $\text{cov}(W_2, p_1)$ is non-zero, so that μ_1/p_2 differs from the ratio of expected marginal utilities, and hence the marginal rate of expected substitution, as the community maximises expected utility. The sign of the covariance, of course, is determined by (7.12) or (7.13).

7.2 Uncertainty and Social Welfare

It should be clear at the outset that social welfare under uncertainty must be lower than the case where the price of the first good is known with certainty to be equal to the mean of the probability distribution of p_1. Given the income constraint, the Pareto optimality condition for welfare maximisation is that the commodity-price ratio be equal to the marginal rate of substitution. This condition is satisfied under certainty conditions, but not in the presence of uncertainty and the non-zero covariance between W_2 and p_1, as is evident from (7.15). It follows then, that social welfare under uncertainty is less than the welfare level attainable under certainty.

A clear-cut demonstration of this point emerges from Fig. 7.1 where the production point is given by P, which is obtained by drawing the internationally determined expected foreign-price line $\bar{F}\bar{P}$ tangential to the transformation curve TT' to reflect the fact that producers are apathetic to risk. The slope of $\bar{F}\bar{P}$ reflects the ratio μ_1/p_2. Suppose the country expects the first good to be the export good and the second good to be the import good, so that the expected consumption point in the free trade equilibrium would lie on $\bar{F}\bar{P}$, to the left of P. Under certainty conditions, the consumption point is given by C and the level of welfare by W_c, with point C satisfying the condition that

E*

$$\frac{E[W_1]}{E[W_2]} = \frac{W_1}{W_2} = \frac{\mu_1}{p_2}.$$

The consumption point under uncertainty, however, is given by U and the welfare level by W_u, with point U satisfying the condition that

$$\frac{E[W_1]}{E[W_2]} \leqslant \frac{\mu_1}{p_2}$$

because here, with $X_1 > C_1$, $\text{cov}(W_2, p_1) = E[W_2(p_1 - \mu_1)] \leqslant 0$ from (7.12).† In the diagram, $E[W_1]/E[W_2]$ is given by the absolute value

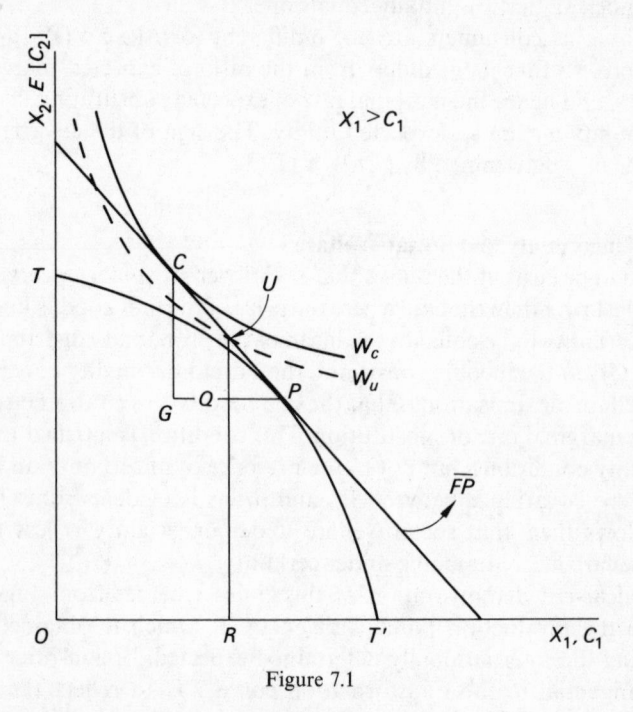

Figure 7.1

of the slope of the social indifference curve W_u at point U. It can be observed that welfare level under uncertainty is lower than the certainty level of welfare. Note that the presence of uncertainty

† Only in the limiting case of risk-neutrality is

$$E[W_2(p_1 - \mu_1)] = 0.$$

leaves the production point unchanged, thereby reflecting risk-apathy on the part of X_1 producers.

There still remains the question of how we determine the expected consumption point U. In the diagram, the community chooses the consumption of the first good at OR, so that the expected consumption of the second good equals UR. This is how the choice of C_1 by the community determines the expected consumption point. Note that if consumers were also apathetic to the risk arising from the randomness of their income, the expected consumption point would be the same as C.

The diagrammatic presentation of the argument yields another interesting result: *The volume of trade under uncertainty is lower than the trade volume in the case where the international price is known with certainty to be equal to the mean of the original distribution.* This follows from the fact that under certainty conditions, the amount of X_1 exported equals GP and the amount of X_2 imported is given by CG, whereas in the presence of uncertainty and the risk-aversion of consumers, the export of X_1 equals $QP < GP$ and the import of X_2 equals $UQ < CG$. Note that in both cases, the actual- or realised-price ratio equals μ_1/p_2; however, in one case it is known, whereas in the other case, it is unknown at the time of decision-making by the community.

The case where the first good is imported is illustrated in Fig. 7.2, where all consumption points lie on $\bar{F}\bar{P}$, to the right of P. The consumption point under uncertainty now reflects that

$$\frac{E[W_1]}{E[W_2]} \geqslant \frac{\mu_1}{p_2}$$

because, in view of (7.13) and (7.14), $\mathrm{cov}\,(W_2, p_1)$ is positive. Thus, the nature of the free trade equilibrium depends on whether X_1 is exported or imported.

Let us now see how an increase in uncertainty affects expected social welfare. As usual, the uncertainty change will be defined in terms of the concept of the mean-preserving spread. Thus, let us write $\hat{p}_1$ as

$$\hat{p}_1 = \gamma p_1 + \theta$$

where $\gamma = 1$ and $\theta = 0$ initially. It may be remembered that an increase in uncertainty is represented by $d\gamma > 0$ along with $d\theta/d\gamma = -\mu_1$.

Replacing p_1 by $\hat{p}_1$ in (7.6) yields

$$E[W] = E[W(C_1, \hat{p}_1 X_1 + X_2 - \hat{p}_1 C_1)]$$

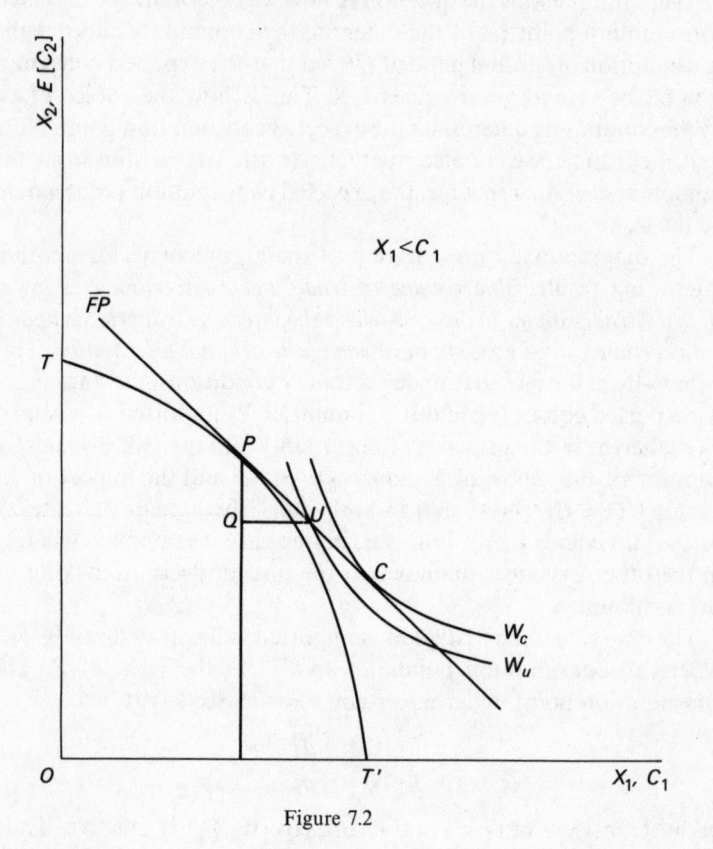

Figure 7.2

where, as before, $p_2 = 1$. Differentiating this with respect to γ and equating $d\theta/d\gamma$ to $-\mu_1$, we obtain

$$\frac{dE[W]}{d\gamma} = E\left[W_1 \frac{dC_1}{d\gamma} + W_2\left\{(X_1 - C_1)(p_1 - \mu_1) - p_1 \frac{dC_1}{d\gamma}\right\}\right]$$

$$= \frac{dC_1}{d\gamma} E[W_1 - p_1 W_2] + (X_1 - C_1) E[W_2(p_1 - \mu_1)].$$

From (7.7), the first term of this expression, in view of $p_2 = 1$, is zero.

Therefore

$$\frac{dE[W]}{d\gamma} = (X_1 - C_1)E[W_2(p_1 - \mu_1)].$$

From (7.12) and (7.13), we know that when $(X_1 - C_1) > 0$, $E[W_2(p_1 - \mu_1)] \leqslant 0$, whereas when $(X_1 - C_1) < 0$, $E[W_2(p_1 - \mu_1)] \geqslant 0$. It follows then that with risk-aversion on the part of the community,

$$\frac{dE[W]}{d\gamma} \leqslant 0.$$

In other words, an increase in uncertainty leads to a decline in expected social welfare, and vice versa.

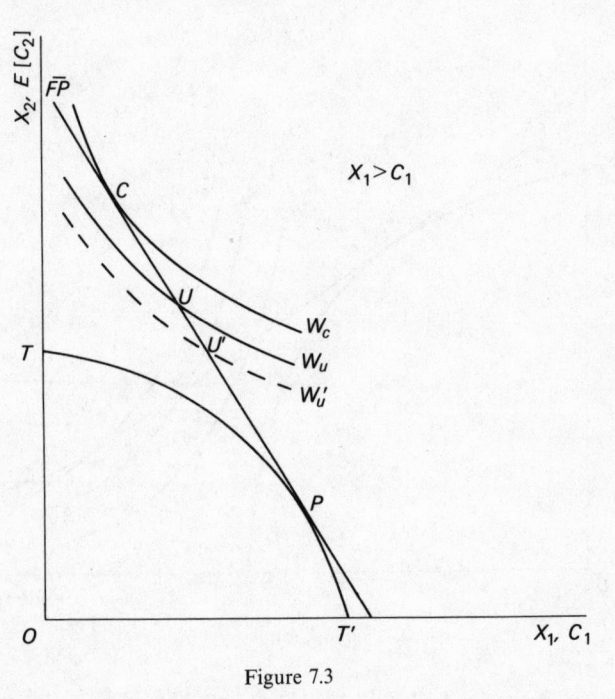

Figure 7.3

A diagrammatic illustration of this result is provided by Fig. 7.3, where the first good is exported. Whatever the level of uncertainty, the production point remains unchanged at P because of our *pro tempore* assumption of risk-neutrality on the part of producers, the consumption point under certainty is C, that under uncertainty is

U with μ_1/p_2 given by the slope of $\overline{F}\overline{P}$. Since U lies to the right of C, it seems natural that an increase in the variance of p_1, with μ_1 unchanged to leave $\overline{F}\overline{P}$ unchanged, will shift the consumption point further to the right, say, to U', so that expected welfare would decline to W_u'.

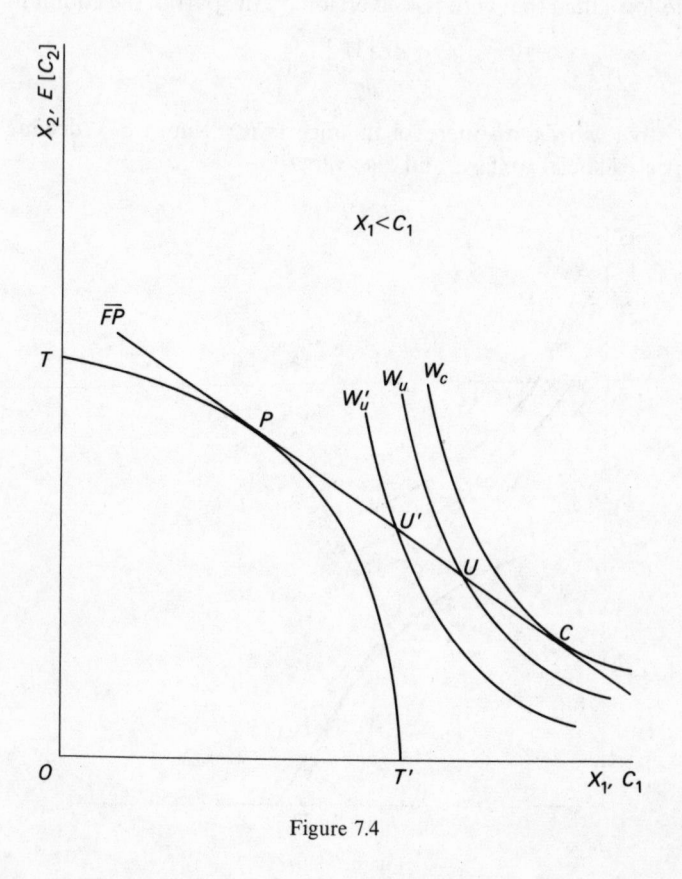

Figure 7.4

A similar explication applies to the case where X_1, as in Fig. 7.4, is the import-competing good. Here, point U is to the left of C and U' is to the left of U'. Once again, W_u' is below W_u to show that an increase in the variance of p_1, with μ_1 unchanged, leads to a decline in expected welfare.

7.3   The General Case

The general case is one where all decision-makers are risk-averters. Here, neither the marginal rate of transformation nor the marginal rate of substitution equal the expected commodity-price ratio. Therefore, social welfare under uncertainty is less than when p_1 is known with certainty to be equal to μ_1 on account of two reasons.

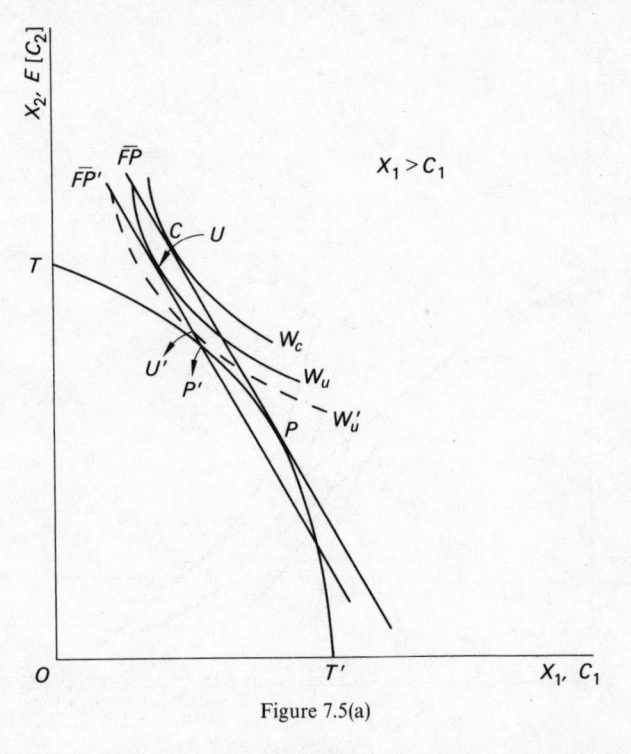

Figure 7.5(a)

In Fig. 7.5, certainty welfare as before is given by W_c, but the level of welfare under uncertainty is given by W_u', which lies below W_c. The production point under uncertainty is P', with $\bar{F}\bar{P}$ parallel to $\bar{F}\bar{P}'$. The total loss in welfare is the sum of two components: The loss in welfare due to risk-aversion of producers can be called the production loss, whereas the loss in welfare from the risk-aversion of consumers can be termed the consumption loss. The production loss is measured by the shift in the social indifference curve from W_c to W_u, whereas the consumption loss is measured by the decline in welfare from W_u to W_u'.

In the case of a rise in uncertainty also, the decline in expected welfare would be twofold; but now risk-aversion alone is not enough to get categorical results. On the production side, we need to assume the hypothesis of non-increasing absolute risk-aversion. Once this assumption is made, the welfare analysis of the preceding chapter can be combined with the analysis of section 7.2 to obtain the

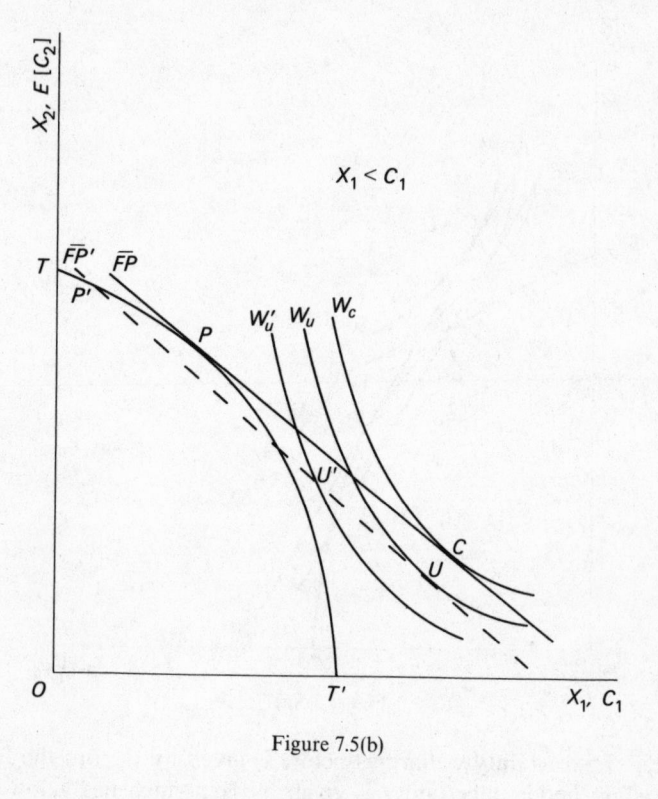

Figure 7.5(b)

suggested result. We can conclude that an increase in uncertainty will increase the production, as well as the consumption loss and hence lead to a twofold loss in expected social welfare.

7.4 Summary

In this chapter, the price-uncertainty model of the preceding chapter was extended to include the social-utility function of the community as well. Uncertainty affects the consumers in so far as their income, equal to the value of production in the economy, becomes uncertain.† The main results of this chapter are as follows:

1. Social welfare under uncertainty is lower than the certainty level of welfare, provided either producers or consumers are not indifferent to risk.
2. The volume of trade under uncertainty is also lower than the corresponding volume under certainty.
3. An increase in uncertainty stimulates a decline in expected social welfare, provided consumers are risk-averse and producers have non-increasing absolute risk-aversion, and conversely.

† For a slightly more general, but also more complicated, formulation of the model developed in this chapter, see Batra and Russell [1]. Some of the issues examined in this chapter have been previously analysed by Brainard and Cooper [2] with the aid of a quadratic social welfare function. Also see Kemp and Liviatan [3] and Turnovsky [4].

REFERENCES

[1] Batra, R. N. and Russell, W. R., 'Gains from Trade Under Uncertainty', *American Economic Review*, forthcoming.
[2] Brainard, W. C. and Cooper, R., 'Uncertainty and Diversification in International Trade', *Food Research Institute Studies in Agricultural Economics, Trade and Development* (Stanford Univ., 1968) 257–85.
[3] Kemp, M. C. and Liviatan, N., 'Production and Trade Patterns Under Uncertainty', *Economic Record* (49 June 1973).
[4] Turnovsky, S. J., 'Technological and Price Uncertainty in a Ricardian Model of International Trade', *Review of Economic Studies*, 41 (Apr 1974) 201–17.

8 Suggestions for Further Research

How much have we accomplished in the preceding chapters in terms of the integration of the available literature on individual economic behaviour under uncertainty with the main corpus of the theory of international trade? Not much by some standards and barely enough by others. For the theory of international trade is a vast subject, its applications are immense, and what has been achieved so far is a bare skeleton in comparison with its enormous potential as a subject for future development.

The presence of international trade in the economy usually contributes to uncertainty in a wide variety of ways, and for this reason, virtually all the theorems obtained from deterministic trade models stand in need of revision. And there is no reason for the researcher to confine attention to blending the tools of probabilistic economics with existing trade models; new ones could be devised where the statistical techniques and stochastic methods are better equipped to handle the problem.

First of all, there are a few results, which I myself should have derived from the models developed in the foregoing chapters, but which, because of my impatience and lengthy mathematical calculations, I have been unable to obtain. For example, the analysis of the Stolper–Samuelson theorem in Chapter 2 needs to be supplemented by a discussion of how a change in the commodity-price ratio affects the expected profits in the first sector. Similarly, the analysis of the commodity-price stabilisation and income distribution in Chapter 6 also can be improved by exploring the implications of a change only in the variance of the probability distribution of international prices for the expected (or even realised) profits of producers facing uncertainty. The expressions that I obtained in this respect allowed little scope for any reasonable interpretation.

The chapter on the gains from trade also needs to be bolstered. There are a number of interesting issues in international welfare economics which deserve comprehensive treatment but were left untouched because of my feeling that the general equilibrium models of production investigated in the earlier chapters are not adequate for this purpose. As far as comparative-statics or positive aspects of trade theory under uncertainty are concerned, these models are quite competent. The introduction of stochastic elements only in one sector keeps the formulation from being too cumbersome, and it still does the job. If, in the interest of generality, uncertainty were introduced in both sectors, the mathematical calculations would perhaps become laborious for even a determined reader. Furthermore, I believe that my results concerning the positive aspects of trade theory will stand up to the test of more complex probings.

The normative side of international trade theory, however, is another matter. When random elements are incorporated only in one sector, they act to create a distortion in the structure of production in that the marginal rate of transformation is no longer equal to the expected-price ratio. The distortion appears to be similar to the one created in certainty models by external diseconomies or economies of scale in one sector or by interindustry factor-price differentials. It is easy to see that the latter type of distortion is different from the one created by uncertainty in one sector, because with uncertainty, the economy still operates on the transformation curve, whereas the factor-price differential not only disrupts the equality between the marginal rate of transformation and the commodity-price ratio, but also leads to a shrinking of the 'efficient' transformation curve towards the origin, so that the production point is no longer on the efficiency locus. Nor is the case of external economies of scale completely analogous with the uncertainty case, because with economies of scale, the unit isoquant of the product in question shifts inwards towards the origin as the output increases, whereas risk-averse behaviour is represented by the opposite, *outward* shift of the unit isoquant. It is the external diseconomies of scale that provide a certainty analogue of the distortion created by risk-averse behaviour in one sector.

In the context of deterministic trade models, it is well known that the equality of the marginal rate of transformation with the commodity-price ratio is crucial for the existence of several theorems in the analysis of gains from trade.† For example, the demonstration

† See Haberler [7] for stating this explicitly.

by Samuelson [15] and Kemp [12] of the superiority, in terms of social welfare, of free trade over no trade depends crucially on this equality. So do Kemp's theorems that some trade is better than no trade and that less restricted trade is superior to more restricted trade. If the marginal rate of transformation does not correspond with the commodity-price ratio, these theorems may not be valid.

If we assume that under uncertainty the community is interested in maximising expected social welfare, it will not be difficult in the context of our uncertainty models to conclude that the conventional hypotheses concerning gains from trade may not hold, for as stated earlier, the marginal rate of transformation in our uncertainty models, expounded in Chapter 7, does not in equilibrium equal the expected-price ratio.

However, treating economic behaviour under uncertainty as a distortion from the normative viewpoint is not a satisfactory method of analysis. Risk-averse behaviour is something natural, something human, and cannot be regarded as an aberration from rational economic behaviour. What we need, therefore, for an unequivocal analysis of the gains from trade under uncertainty is a framework which, in the presence of rational economic behaviour under uncertainty, is capable of generating the correspondence between the marginal rate of transformation and the expected commodity-price ratio.

In what follows, I present a framework and the condition in which this may be true, but unfortunately I have not been able to interpret this condition in any appealing way. I will, of course, suggest some possible interpretations which are perhaps valid, but I have not been able to furnish rigorous proofs of my assertions.

What I propose to do is to devise a framework, where prices of both goods are uncertain and all producers have to make their input–output decisions on the basis of the probability distributions of the two prices. As usual, the two production functions are given by

$$X_1 = F_1(K_1, L_1) \tag{8.1}$$

and

$$X_2 = F_2(K_2, L_2). \tag{8.2}$$

With producers in both sectors taking factor prices as given, the expected utility from profits in the ith sector is maximised by equating

$$E[U_i'(\pi_i)(p_i F_{Li} - w)]$$

and

$$E[U_i'(\pi_i)(p_i F_{Ki} - r)]$$

to zero, where $\pi_i = p_i X_i - wL_i - rK_i$ is the profit in the ith sector, and $U_i' = dU_i/d\pi_i$ is the marginal utility from profit in the ith sector. Factor rewards are still the same in both sectors. The first-order conditions for expected utility maximisation then yield

$$w = \frac{E[U_1' p_1]}{E[U_1']} F_{L1} = \frac{E[U_2' p_2]}{E[U_2']} F_{L2} \tag{8.3}$$

and

$$r = \frac{E[U_1' p_1]}{E[U_1']} F_{K1} = \frac{E[U_2' p_2]}{E[U_2']} F_{K2}. \tag{8.4}$$

Finally, the full-employment equations continue to be given by

$$L_1 + L_2 = L \tag{8.5}$$

and

$$K_1 + K_2 = K. \tag{8.6}$$

Differentiating (8.1) and (8.2) totally, we obtain

$$\frac{dX_1}{dX_2} = \frac{F_{K1} dK_1 + F_{L1} dL_1}{F_{K2} dK_2 + F_{L2} dL_2}$$

which, in view of (8.3) and (8.4) and the full-employment conditions, becomes

$$\frac{dX_1}{dX_2} = -\frac{E[U_2' p_2] E[U_1']}{E[U_1' p_1] E[U_2']} \tag{8.7}$$

$$= -\frac{E[U_1']\{E[U_2']\mu_2 + \sigma_2\}}{E[U_2']\{E[U_1']\mu_1 + \sigma_1\}} \tag{8.8}$$

where μ_i is the expected price of the ith good, and σ_i is the covariance between U_i' and p_i. For risk-averse firms, $\sigma_i < 0$.

From (8.8), it is clear that in general dX_1/dX_2 is not equal to the expected-price ratio because $\sigma_i < 0$. The condition which will achieve this equality is given by

$$\frac{E[U_1']\{E[U_2']\mu_2 + \sigma_2\}}{E[U_2']\{E[U_1']\mu_1 + \sigma_1\}} = \frac{\mu_2}{\mu_1}$$

or by

$$\frac{\sigma_1}{\mu_1 E[U_1']} = \frac{\sigma_2}{\mu_2 E[U_2']}. \tag{8.9}$$

The derivation of this condition, ostensibly enough, is not difficult in spite of the presence of stochastic elements in both sectors, but its interpretation is not straightforward, at least at first glance. The condition does reveal an element of symmetry. For the marginal rate of transformation to be equal to the expected-price ratio, the covariance divided by the product of the expected price and the expected value of the marginal utility from profits should be the same in both sectors.

Can we accord to this condition any interpretation based on rational economic behaviour? My feeling is that there must be one, but I myself am unable to put my finger on it. Perhaps the condition implies that in equilibrium the marginal rate of risk-premium is the same in both sectors, where the risk-premium is normally defined as the difference between the expected return from the risky prospect and its certainty equivalent. The risk-premium is positive for the risk-averter, zero for one indifferent to risk, and negative for the risk-preferer. The sign of σ_i, after all, is related to the concept of the risk-premium, which is positive, negative, or zero when σ_i is negative, positive, or zero. It is easy to justify the statement that in equilibrium the risk-premium of producers in each sector should be the same at the margin, much like the fact that in the certainty equilibrium the value of each factor's productivity at the margin is the same in both sectors. The argument is that if the marginal risk-premiums are not the same everywhere, producers will move from the more risky to the less risky sector, and this movement in a stable two-sector economy will generate the desired equalisation.

Perhaps the condition given by (8.9) implies that the rate of expected profits is the same in both industries, because when $\sigma_i < 0$, the expected profit in each sector is positive. One thing is clear. Condition (8.9) cannot be satisfied if producers in both sectors do not have the same attitude towards risk. That situation, of course, would be a genuine distortion in the productive structure of the economy.

The reader may raise a legitimate question at this point. How can we utilise the two-sector model with uncertainty in both sectors when it has already been rejected mainly on grounds of its intractability? The reason for my advocacy of this model now is that first it may do the job, and second, the analysis of normative aspects of economic theory under uncertainty does not usually involve the same degree of complexity as do the positive aspects. This at least has been my experience in my investigation of the economic issues under uncertainty.

Finally, in the analysis of the gains from trade under uncertainty, we have to cope with the problems arising from the inequality of the expected-price ratio with the marginal rate of substitution, for the theorems by Kemp and Samuelson may still not hold even if the marginal rate of transformation corresponds with the expected-price ratio. This problem can be very simply resolved by making the reasonable assumption that consumption decisions can be postponed until after the resolution of actual prices. This way, uncertainty becomes irrelevant to the consumption decisions. Note that such an assumption cannot be maintained in the case of production, which normally requires commitments by producers to hire inputs and produce goods in advance of the knowledge of actual prices.

Until now, I have indicated the need for reformulation under uncertainty for those problems which have hitherto been investigated in terms of deterministic trade models. A few words may now be said about some problems which can be handled only with the aid of the tools of probabilistic economics.

The lifeline in many developed countries depends on imports of raw materials and other primary products to be used for further production of manufactured goods. What happens in the economy if the foreign supply of such goods becomes unreliable and thus becomes the cause of uncertainty in the availability of some inputs?† A number of interesting questions merit serious investigation. How does the economy in general respond to this type of uncertainty? Do producers respond by substituting the securely available inputs

---

† The existence of international trade in cotton is a case in point. Several developed, as well as underdeveloped, countries have highly developed textile industries, but not all of them produce sufficient cotton at home, and thus they have to import it from abroad. However, the production of cotton almost everywhere is subject to the vagaries of weather, and this imparts an element of uncertainty to the foreign supply.

for the uncertain inputs, thereby causing a decline in imports of such products? In general, what implications does this phenomenon have for the theory of effective protection, which takes into account the tariffs on final, as well as intermediate products?

Issues become more complicated when the introduction of a policy itself becomes the source of uncertainty. The 10 per cent import surcharge imposed by President Nixon in August 1971 led to widespread uncertainty all over the world about the very future of international commerce.

It is possible to conceive of cases where the prime source of uncertainty is the presence of international trade. For example, under the flexible exchange standard, exchange-rate fluctuations lead to fluctuations in domestic-currency prices and may thus generate uncertainty for the producers. This will happen in spite of stability in the international prices of the goods. Since this type of uncertainty is not present in a closed economy where exchange rates are irrelevant, a question may be raised as to whether the introduction of trade contributes to an improvement in social welfare, because with trade, welfare may be subjected to two conflicting pulls, one tending to raise it, and the other tending to lower it.

Until now, my concern has been with suggesting further avenues of research in the regime of the theory of international trade. In fact, the general equilibrium models developed in the preceding chapters can be fruitfully utilised in the analysis of several other areas of economic theory. Perhaps all the problems that have been customarily analysed in terms of the two-sector certainty models can also be investigated in terms of our stochastic models, because, in general, uncertainty influences most modes of economic behaviour. Like the deterministic two-sector models, the models developed in this book have enough resilience that they can be modified, if necessary, to deal with the problem at hand.†

So far, the deterministic two-sector model of production has been applied to the analysis of problems in (a) public finance (see Harberger [8], Wells [17] and Johnson [10], among others), (b) the theory of labour (Johnson and Mieszkowski [11], Magee [13], Jones [9], Batra and Pattanaik [3], among others), (c) the theory of growth (see Uzawa [16], Drandakis [5] and Batra [1], among many others), (d) the theory of industrial location (see McClure [14], (e) monetary

† In this connection, see Batra [2], where the general equilibrium model of Chapter 2 is applied to investigate the incidence of corporation income-tax.

theory (see Foley and Sidrauski [6]), and finally, (f) regional economics (see Batra and Scully [4]). There perhaps are some other applications that may have escaped my attention.

It is worth noting again that the general equilibrium models developed in this book can also be applied to the investigation of all these problems. It will be interesting to see whether the customary results continue to hold in the presence of uncertainty. The reader may also be interested in obtaining additional specifications that may be needed to uphold the conventional results.

REFERENCES

[1] Batra, R. N., 'Monopoly Theory in General Equilibrium and the Two-Sector Model of Economic Growth', *Journal of Economic Theory*, 4 (June 1972) 355–71.

[2] ——, 'A General Equilibrium Model of the Incidence of Corporation Income Tax Under Uncertainty', Working Paper No. 33, Department of Economics, Southern Methodist University.

[3] ——, and Pattanaik, P. K., 'Factor Market Imperfections, the Terms of Trade, and Welfare', *American Economic Review*, 61 (Dec 1971) 946–55.

[4] ——, and Scully, Gerald W., 'Technical Progress, Economic Growth, and the North-South Wage Differential', *Journal of Regional Science*, 12 (Dec 1972) 375–386.

[5] Drandakis, E. M., 'Factor Substitution in the Two-Sector Growth Model', *Review of Economic Studies*, 30 (Oct 1963) 217–228.

[6] Foley, Duncan K., and Sidrauski, Miguel, *Monetary and Fiscal Policy in a Growing Economy* (New York: Macmillan, 1971).

[7] Haberler, G., 'Some Problems in the Pure Theory of International Trade', *Economic Journal*, 60 (June 1950) 223–40.

[8] Harberger, A. C., 'The Incidence of the Corporation Income Tax', *Journal of Political Economy*, 70 (June 1962) 215–40.

[9] Jones, R. W., 'Distortions in Factor Markets and the General Equilibrium Model of Production', *Journal of Political Economy*, 79 (May–June 1971) 437–59.

[10] Johnson, H. G., 'General Equilibrium Analysis of Excise Taxes: Comment', *American Economic Review*, 46 (Mar 1956) 151–56.

[11] Johnson, H. G., and Mieszkowski, P. M., 'The Effects of Unionization on the Distribution of Income: A General Equilibrium Approach', *Quarterly Journal of Economics*, 84 (Nov 1970) 539–61.

[12] Kemp, M. C., *The Pure Theory of International Trade* (New Jersey: Prentice-Hall, 1964).

[13] Magee, S. P., 'Factor Market Distortions, Production, Distribution and the Pure Theory of International Trade', *Quarterly Journal of Economics*, 85 (Nov 1971) 623–43.

[14] McClure, C. E., 'Taxation, Substitution, and Industrial Location', *Journal of Political Economy*, 78 (1970) 112–32.

[15] Samuelson, P. A., 'The Gains from International Trade', *Canadian Journal of Economics and Political Science*, 5 (May 1939) 195–205.

[16] Uzawa, H., 'On a Two-Sector Model of Economic Growth', *Review of Economic Studies*, 29 (Oct 1961) 40–47.

[17] Wells, Paul, 'A General Equilibrium Analysis of Excise Taxes', *American Economic Review*, 45 (June 1955) 345–59.

Author Index

Subject Index